The Secrets o

Make Your Life Happily

Alice Hey

Copyright © 2023 by Alice Hey

All rights reserved.

No portion of this book may be reproduced in any form without written permission from the publisher or author, except as permitted by U.S. copyright law.

This publication is designed to provide accurate and authoritative information in regard to the subject matter covered. It is sold with the understanding that neither the author nor the publisher is engaged in rendering legal, investment, accounting or other professional services. While the publisher and author have used their best efforts in preparing this book, they make no representations or warranties with respect to the accuracy or completeness of the contents of this book and specifically disclaim any implied warranties of merchantability or fitness for a particular purpose. No warranty may be created or extended by sales representatives or written sales materials. The advice and strategies contained herein may not be suitable for your situation. You should consult with a professional when appropriate. Neither the publisher nor the author shall be liable for any loss of profit or any other commercial damages, including but not limited to special, incidental, consequential, personal, or other damages.

Table of Contents

INTRODUCTION 3
CHAPTER ONE 4
   Let's Go Back to the Roots. 4
   Behavioral Strategies: The Tale of Chris and Jim. 14
CHAPTER TWO 16
   Roots That Influence the Future. 16
   Psychological Defense Mechanisms and Their Role in Jim's Behavior. 23
CHAPTER TREE 25
   Where Does Self-Confidence Come From? 25
   Where Does Confidence Come From? 33
CHAPTER FOUR 40
   Taking Destiny into Our Hands. 40
   Subchapter One 40
   Subchapter Two 45
   Too Heavy to Bear. 45
CHAPTER FIVE 65
   Practical Intelligence and the Tipping Point Effect. 65
CHAPTER SIX 83
   The Magic Mirror: Who's Beside Us. 83
CHAPTER SEVEN 94
   Never Settle for What You've Achieved. What Might Hold You Back on the Path to Success? 94
   Prisoners of Our Own Convictions: How Our Limitations Stifle Growth. 98
CHAPTER EIGHT 111
   Unwritten Traditions 111
   Assertive Communication. 118
CHAPTER NINE 121
   Artificial Surplus. 121
CHAPTER TEN 126
   The Power of Unity. 126
   Human as a Social Animal. 132
Let's Summarize 137

INTRODUCTION

Reflect on this: have there been times in your life when circumstances seemed to conspire against you for no apparent reason? Have there been moments when your decisions, your behavior — including hesitation or inaction, as well as proactive steps — led to disappointments? Yet, at the same time, others seemed to effortlessly find success and everything appeared to go their way.

Many would resonate with these scenarios. Many may not even realize that their ineffective behaviors might be playing such recurring tricks on them.

Our intention here isn't to judge or point fingers at those who've faced challenges to mock their setbacks. The aim of our conversation is to shift your behaviors, transform your perspectives on life, and elevate your efficacy. I've walked this path countless times, beginning with my own journey and extending to my work with individuals who sought this kind of guidance.

Now, it's your turn to evolve for the better, to join a group of individuals for whom success and happiness are natural states. Their behaviors are aligned in such a way that the outcomes of their actions almost always yield success.

I'm honored to have the opportunity to assist you in this transformation. Let's embark on our journey together.

CHAPTER ONE

Let's Go Back to the Roots.

Two different tales about the same thing.

On a sunny summer day, when Chris was 7 years old, he was playing in the yard of his house. Nearby, two adults sat on a bench discussing the latest match of the local soccer team. Chris, having attended soccer training for six months already, decided to share his views. He approached the adults, introduced himself, and confidently shared his perspective on the game. They were pleasantly surprised by the boy's reasoning.

Chris was fortunate to be born into a middle-class family. His parents cared for him and prioritized his upbringing, enrolling him in various sports and creative activities. One time, Chris failed a math test at school. This was unusual for him because, despite his active participation in numerous extracurricular activities, he was typically successful academically. Recognizing that just overlooking the failure would be a mistake for Chris, his mother decided to intervene.

The day after Chris showed her his grade, she went to the school. Meeting with the math teacher, she expressed gratitude for his efforts, then got to her request. "You know, I believe every student deserves a second chance. Chris admitted he didn't prepare well for this test due to his extracurricular commitments. But he's willing to put in more time studying and would like a chance to retake the test," she said.

The teacher looked at her, thoughtfully nodded, and replied, "You know, I'm always ready to support students who genuinely want to improve. If Chris is truly willing to dedicate extra time to his studies, I'll allow him to retake the test."

His parents backed him up at home, always checking in on his progress with coaches, and communicating with teachers about his academic performance. They would ask for retake opportunities when needed, instilling an understanding of the importance of taking responsibility for mistakes and the possibility of rectifying them.

On one fine Sunday, Chris's father decided to tend to the garden surrounding their home. He invited Chris to assist him.

"Chris, if you help me weed the beds and plant new flowers, I'll give you something special," said his father with a smile.

Knowing his father always kept his promises, Chris agreed. They spent the entire day working together: weeding, planting, and watering. It was hard work, but Chris felt a sense of accomplishment.

By evening, when the job was done, his father handed Chris a beautiful airplane model that the boy had long desired.

"You've earned this, Chris," his father said, hugging his son. "Hard work is an important trait. If you work diligently and strive towards your goals, you'll always be rewarded."

Chris's parents instilled a work ethic in him, incentivizing him with rewards for tasks completed. Whether it was school or chores at home, he always approached them diligently and, whenever possible, saw them to completion.

From a young age, Chris's parents put a premium on his health. They always emphasized that health was the foundation of a successful and happy life. At the age of 12, Chris began to notice his eyes getting tired after prolonged reading. Since he always had an open line of communication with his parents, he immediately informed them about this. Rather than dismissing the issue, his parents decided to see an optometrist.

On the way to the doctor's office, Chris's mom turned on the radio to his favorite station and started a conversation: "Chris, do you remember how your dad and I always told you that you should take care of your health?"

Chris nodded, enjoying the music.

"Let's think about what questions you'll ask the doctor. These are your eyes, and it's important for you to be involved in the treatment process."

Chris thought, "I wonder why my eyes get tired so quickly. And what are the ways to fix it."

"Great!" smiled mom. "You should also ask about lenses or glasses that can help. And don't forget to express your wishes regarding eye comfort."

When they arrived at the optometrist's, Chris was ready. He confidently began the conversation, asking the doctor questions they had discussed. He described his symptoms precisely and in detail, expressed concern about preserving his vision, and inquired about recommendations and possible solutions.

The doctor was surprised and at the same time impressed by Chris's confidence and responsibility. Instead of only addressing his mom, as is often the case with children, the optometrist actively engaged with Chris, answering his questions and providing information. Chris's mom proudly watched her son, pleased that he was learning to take responsibility for his health.

When the doctor suggested certain lenses, Chris inquired about their benefits and also expressed a desire to find ones that would reduce eye fatigue when reading.

On the way home, mom said, "Today you showed that you know how to take care of your health. This is a very important skill, Chris."

The Secrets of Living

Once, when Chris was about 14 years old, his parents decided to replace the old garage with a new one. They thought it would be an excellent way to teach Chris practical communication skills, especially with older people.

Chris's father suggested he talk to a local garage builder. "Chris, this is your project. You will conduct the negotiations, and I will be there to support you," he said.

Arriving at the location, Chris was a bit nervous. But, remembering his father's support, he took a deep breath and approached the master. "Hello, I need a new garage. What can you offer?", Chris began.

The master, surprised by the boy's confidence, presented several options. Instead of immediately agreeing, Chris asked questions about the materials, timelines, and costs. He expressed his preferences regarding the garage's design and size. These details had been previously discussed with his father, who had advised Chris on how the negotiations might proceed and what specifics to clarify.

At one point, the builder tried to propose a more expensive option. But Chris, knowing the budget set by his father, politely and firmly steered the conversation back: "We are looking for a quality, yet budget-friendly option. What else can you offer in this range?"

By the end of the meeting, the builder had agreed to Chris's terms, and a deal was made. Chris's father was proud and said, "Son, you did a great job. You were persistent and spoke on equal terms. If we hadn't liked the conditions, we would've turned to another professional. Soon we'll be using the new garage that you ordered."

This experience was a real lesson for Chris. He realized that even being young, one could achieve communication goals by being confident, clear, and persistent.

His parents taught him the same values their own parents had instilled in them: to communicate with peers and elders as equals and to express their wishes, steering conversations in a direction that addresses their concerns.

When Chris was 12, his mother suggested he take dance lessons. "It will complement your athletic build, and you'll learn how to interact with girls," she explained.

The initial lessons were challenging. Not every boy finds it easy to overcome their shyness and take a girl by the hand. But with the constant support of his parents and an experienced teacher, Chris grew more confident.

Chris quickly realized that dancing was not just about beautiful movements; it was about sensing your partner, adapting to their rhythm, and leading them through the dance. These skills translated well into his everyday life. Chris became more confident interacting with the opposite gender, attracting many female friends who admired his grace, self-assurance, and tact.

By the time Chris reached his senior years in school, he was the shining star of school dance events. Girls would practically line up for the chance to dance with him. Yet, Chris remained as kind-hearted and attentive as he had always been.

Those dance lessons did more than just elevate Chris's popularity among the girls. They imparted invaluable life lessons about communication, self-confidence, and understanding the opposite gender.

Naturally, he grew up as a self-assured young man, equipped with a myriad of skills from various activities. He understood the basics of teamwork; stressful situations didn't faze him, as he calmly addressed and, where possible, turned them to his advantage. Chris knew what he wanted and was adept at expressing his desires

He sidestepped conflicts, seeing no reason to get involved. He was never hesitant to address problems, having been trained to believe that most of them are solvable.

After successfully graduating from university, Chris began his job search. He had a clear plan and confidence in his capabilities. Within just two weeks, Chris received an offer from a major company in the city center.

From day one on the job, Chris stood out as a responsible and proactive employee. His colleagues quickly recognized his communicative nature and professionalism. He actively participated in corporate events, business lunches, and training sessions. Chris easily built rapport with every member of the team, whether it was his direct supervisor or the security guard at the entrance.

A few months into his role, Chris had seamlessly integrated into the company culture. His charisma and teamwork skills made him indispensable. He was always ready to help, back an initiative, or suggest a solution to a challenging problem.

Furthermore, the collaborative atmosphere at the company allowed Chris to effortlessly make new friends among his colleagues. Most of them were just as upbeat and ambitious as he was. Together, they spent time after work, held picnics over the weekends, and traveled on vacations.

Chris felt he was right where he belonged. He was content, doing what he loved surrounded by wonderful people. All in all, he was truly enjoying life.

Upon learning of his son's poor grades, the father became upset, and a huge argument nearly erupted at home. In the end, the father told Jim that he needed to study harder if he cared about his future. Instead of feeling supported, Jim felt it was better not to discuss his problems with his parents if it only stressed them out and offered no help. He felt alone with his challenges. It seemed that his parents not only didn't help but added more pressure by imposing their own insecurities and fear of having to address the issue. It was as if teachers were big and intimidating bosses they dared not confront. As if any problem was solely Jim's responsibility, and they were deeply saddened and fearful that they might have to address it. They were afraid to express their opinions and desires; they silently endured all misfortunes, quietly towards outsiders, but venting their stress and fear on the weakest at home.

This wasn't the first time something like this happened. Jim was finishing the first grade and had become accustomed to such reactions from his parents. This time he didn't want to show them his grades, but with the academic year ending, they decided to check on their own. Notably, they never offered to help with his studies or communication with peers or teachers. Jim took this for granted; he didn't know any different and believed it was the only way.

The sun was shining brightly when the family turned on the sports channel in Jim's house. The baseball final was on, and every family member watched the game with interest. Though only seven, Jim was glued to the screen, keenly observing every move of the players. The triumphant home-run, impressive throws, and tense moments made an indelible impression on him.

The next day, playing outside, Jim saw some older neighborhood kids excitedly discussing the previous day's match. He wanted to join and share how captivating the game was for him, but shyness and fear that the older kids wouldn't care about his opinion held him back.

Standing aside, Jim listened as the kids enthusiastically recalled the game's highlights, made bets on upcoming matches, and discussed players' techniques. He yearned to join the familiar faces of the neighborhood kids in their conversation, but he kept his distance, pretending to be engrossed in his toys.

From a young age, Jim often heard adults say, "Children should be seen and not heard." Even though no one ever voiced it directly, many adults around him gave the impression that his opinions didn't matter.

In Jim's family, his desires were rarely considered. Whether it was choosing dinner or picking a movie for family night, decisions were made without considering the boy's input. When Jim timidly tried to express his views among peers or teachers, he was often ignored or interrupted, and frankly, he didn't attempt it very often.

After watching a baseball match, Jim felt a strong desire to start training. He was inspired by the competitive spirit, the players' teamwork, and their drive to win. He shared this dream with his father, hoping for support, his voice tinged with excitement.

However, his father was adamant, "Baseball training is expensive, and I doubt you'd excel. You know we don't have the extra money for such luxuries." These words deeply hurt Jim. It pained him to realize that even his dearest dreams couldn't become reality because of his family's lack of faith in him. For the next few days, the family discussed Jim's desire to train. His father mockingly suggested that Jim probably imagined himself as a great baseball player, while his mother subtly chuckled.

As the years went by, Jim learned to keep his dreams and desires to himself, striving not to draw attention.

For the upcoming school year, Jim's parents decided to buy him new clothes. All year, he had dreamed of the stylish jacket and jeans he saw in store windows and on his classmates. However, when the family arrived at the store, his dreams quickly crumbled.

Jim's mother held out a swamp-green jacket with outdated patterns and plain, drab-colored jeans. "We can't afford expensive clothes," she said, "these will do for a year until you outgrow them."

Jim's heart sank. He tried to politely object: "Mom, can we maybe look for something else? I'm afraid I'll get teased at school wearing these."

Jim's father replied firmly, "We can't spend more than we have. You're growing quickly, and in a year, we'll have to buy you new clothes again."

The next day at school, Jim faced the ridicule and mockery of his classmates. He felt ashamed and hurt. He understood his parents were doing their best, but the feeling of humiliation was overpowering. Jim tried to avoid attention, hid from the jeers, and bitterly endured each day.

One particular school day began especially rough for Jim. Even before classes started, as Jim played in the yard with other kids, Mr. Gray, the school janitor, approached him. In Mr. Gray's hands was an overturned chair with an obscene drawing on it.

"Was this you?" he asked sternly, staring intently at Jim.

Jim was in shock; he hadn't even seen that chair before. "No, I... it wasn't me," he stammered, feeling his knees go weak.

The Secrets of Living

But his feeble objections were instantly dismissed. Someone amongst the gathering crowd suggested Jim was likely the culprit. "I thought you were different," Mr. Gray remarked, "I hope you get what's coming to you."

Jim felt humiliated in front of the entire school. He understood that, despite his innocence, his reputation had been tarnished, feeling utterly powerless even when he was right. On his way home, he pondered how to explain the situation to his parents, but words failed him.

That evening, when his parents learned of the incident, their faces turned ashen. His mother sighed, and his father stayed silent, casting a stern look at his son. It seemed they too believed their son was guilty. Or perhaps they just didn't want to confront the school administration.

Jim felt abandoned and misunderstood. It was hard for him to accept that he was injustly accused, and that no one tried to defend him.

By age 14, Jim's already challenging life grew even more difficult. His lack of self-confidence made interactions with girls tough. His parents would tell him that it would get better with time, but that was of little comfort to Jim. While his friends tried to woo the girls, Jim stayed on the sidelines, pretending he wasn't interested.

Coincidentally, Jim became fascinated with graffiti. He loved the craft: the sense of freedom, the adrenaline rush when drawing something forbidden on city walls. But one day, he went too far, leaving a mark in the city's central square.

He was caught by the police.

A storm broke out at home. His parents were livid. His father, shaking his head, said, "Did you decide to become a criminal? You're heading nowhere, just creating problems!" His mother, in tears, lamented, "We tried to give you everything, and this is how you repay us?". The family paid the fine. Mr. Gray, the school janitor, dryl[y] remarked that he had identified the troublemaker long before the police did.

Jim felt that attending college was his opportunity to turn over a new leaf. But prestigious education was out of reach; his family couldn't afford it, and his grade[s] didn't qualify him for any scholarships. So, he enrolled in a free community college[.] However, his time there didn't unfold as he'd hoped. The courses were tough[,] studying became a struggle, and he felt out of place among the other students. A[s] weeks turned into months, his passion for learning dwindled.

After flunking a significant test, Jim's professor called him into his office[,] genuinely wanting to help. The professor offered him extra tutoring sessions t[o] prepare for a retake. But Jim declined.

"Professor, you don't get it," Jim began, "This academic stuff isn't for me. It's fo[r] nerds who bury themselves in books all day and night. I've chosen a different path."

The professor sighed, gazing at the young man before him. "Jim, all I want is fo[r] you to reach your potential. But the choice is yours," he said, attempting to mask hi[s] disappointment.

In the end, before he could be dismissed for his poor performance, Jim decided t[o] drop out.

Behavioral Strategies: The Tale of Chris and Jim.

Every individual is akin to a unique book, penned by multiple authors: thei[r] parents, environment, education, and themselves. Let's delve into the contrasting tales of Chris and Jim to understand the factors that mold behavioral strategies and the consequences of choosing specific paths.

Chris was fortunate to grow up with parents who constantly supported him, motivating his achievements with rewards and praise. They cultivated an environment where he felt valued and significant. This nurturing gave rise to Chris's strong self-worth, which subsequently became the foundation of his self-confidence.

Contrastingly, Jim's upbringing was marred by uncertainty and a glaring lack of support. This resulted in him developing an avoidance strategy. He learned to conceal his feelings, withhold his opinions, and sidestep potential confrontations.

In psychology, there's a term called "locus of control". If someone has an internal locus of control, they believe they have the capability to steer their life and achieve success. Chris exemplifies this. On the other hand, Jim's external locus of control makes him feel that he's at the mercy of circumstances.

Cognitive distortions also play a role here. Confronted with failures, Jim generalized his experiences, thinking, "I'm a mess; I'll never amount to anything." This is a classic case of overgeneralization. Chris, on the flip side, attributed his successes to his personal attributes rather than external factors.

It's essential to recognize that behavioral strategies aren't immutable traits we're born with. They're a set of responses shaped by the world around us and our experiences within it. With this knowledge, we can channel our behaviors constructively, refining our personal and communicative skills. It's crucial to underline that it's never too late to alter one's strategy and embark on a fresh chapter in life. Human psychological flexibility empowers us to learn, adapt, and evolve, even if our past narratives suggested otherwise.

CHAPTER TWO

Roots That Influence the Future.

In essence, our lives can be likened to a loop of time. It's as if we live the same day repeatedly, in a metaphorical sense. The patterns of our behavior, our reactions to stimuli, and the actions we take to satisfy our needs and desires, represent consistent strategies.

We tackle problems and challenges in very similar ways over time. By analyzing our actions in comparable situations, we can discern the pattern or template we're operating under. While some of these patterns prove effective almost always, others falter.

Once we recognize a pattern, be it an ineffective one that needs refining, or a productive one that should be solidified, we've taken the first and pivotal step towards improvement.

At its core, there are only actions and reactions. Just as we execute actions and yield specific reactions or outcomes, external influences can act upon us, triggering a particular response. This response is not random. It's conditioned by our environment and past experiences.

To evaluate our actions and reactions, we need to comprehend their sequence and rationale. Without understanding, transformation remains elusive.

In simpler terms, if you infuse a single day with most of your activities, you'll swiftly see the resemblance of that day to the entirety of your life. We provide consistent reactions. In fact, this day essentially mirrors the time loop we're ensnared in.

The Secrets of Living

Often, individuals are compelled to break their behavioral patterns through sheer will, usually prompted by a stern external reality check. Your inherent needs are unlikely to change abruptly, and you've adjusted to living with them. The same goes for all reaction templates. We perceive them as a natural state of affairs.

On the one hand, this allows for automatic actions, conserving mental energy. After repeated execution, an action becomes ingrained and natural. On the other hand, the deeply rooted nature of these actions makes it challenging to disrupt an ineffective pattern. Primarily, this is due to the difficulty in distinguishing it amidst the backdrop of its ubiquity.

Once we've identified these patterns, it's imperative to make a conscious effort to redirect them towards a more favorable outcome. Through repetition, we can solidify these improved behaviors until they become second nature. Interestingly, individuals who frequently encounter stressful situations and manage to derive a benefit from them eventually don't perceive these events as stressors.

So, let's transform our typical day into one that's more productive, fulfilling, and beneficial in every aspect.

Acquiring and refining effective skills, and eliminating the ineffective ones, is essentially the purpose of life and the key to genuine happiness.

College events often pave the way for new friendships. On one such evening, Jim stood by the bar, drink in hand, when he noticed a girl with bright, shoulder-length hair and blue eyes approaching him, her face adorned with a smile.

"Hi, are you Jim?" she began, "I'm Linda. I noticed you during the art history lecture."

Caught slightly off guard but pleasantly surprised, Jim started chatting with her. To his astonishment, they had a lot in common. Soft music played in the background, casting a cozy ambiance. The two settled comfortably at the bar, initiating their conversation with casual college banter.

"Do you attend art classes?" Linda asked.

"Well, I occasionally drop by," admitted Jim. "Art helps me unwind and alleviate stress. Have you ever tried painting?"

"Yes, I have an entire display of my works at home," Linda replied. "I try to channel my emotions through paint and canvas."

Their talk gradually deepened. Jim opened up about his childhood, sharing stories of struggles with peers and how art served as his refuge.

"I've had my share of self-doubt too," Linda confessed. "But art has been my salvation. When I paint, I feel like I can truly be myself."

"I've found that art provides me with a freedom of expression that I often miss in daily life," Jim shared.

The evening seemed to be ushering in a fresh start for Jim when Linda, looking directly into his eyes, said, "I've recently finished a few paintings. Would you like to see them?"

Instead of feeling joy or curiosity, Jim was overtaken by a sudden tension. Past experiences had often taught him that people might want to mock or ridicule him. "She probably just wants to make fun of me," he thought.

"You know," he said, a chill in his voice, "I think I'll leave. I've had enough of art and paintings for today. Thanks for the company."

Linda stood perplexed, watching him leave. Her genuine interest in Jim was heartfelt.

The Secrets of Living

Whatever we engage in, we improve that skill. Thus, to acquire a skill, we need to repeat it several times, ideally stimulated by rewards. In other words, if we idle, it provides fertile ground for solidifying that habit, a primitive incentive in the absence of immediate stress.

Regrettably, not everyone is fortunate enough to be born and raised in a conducive environment. It's a fact of life. Such a situation has many downsides. For instance, if you've been in an "aggressive" setting, you're likely to have developed negative reflexes—expecting toxic and aggressive influences and reacting defensively to such triggers.

Later on, when someone offers something positive, you're braced for negativity, immediately on guard. This repels people and potential joys from your life. It's also worth noting that you might not know how to express your emotions and desires, having conditioned yourself to believe they're irrelevant.

Reflect on this: If changes in your past have primarily been for the worse, would you look forward to or strive for upcoming changes?

If your experiences mainly involved being mocked or belittled, would you be receptive to new interactions?

The answer is evident. If past experiences were predominantly negative, they shape one's expectations and mindset. Changes that brought grief in the past are perceived as potential threats in the future. Similarly, if someone was consistently belittled during interactions, they'd likely be wary of new social engagements, fearing a repeat of past traumas.

Jim grew up in an environment where his opinions were seldom valued. In a family that often overlooked or dismissed his feelings and needs, he faced his initial barriers in communication and self-expression. A lack of support and consistent failures at school cultivated in him a low self-worth.

One of the pivotal moments in Jim's life was being denied college admission on scholarship due to poor academic performance. Lacking the necessary confidence and self-sufficiency, he didn't even attempt to take advantage of the help offered to him by a professor.

Jim's social relationships were also complicated. Due to past experiences where he felt vulnerable and subjected to ridicule, Jim couldn't correctly interpret friendly gestures, as was the case with Linda. His behavior was driven by psychological defense mechanisms, such as denial and projection, which he employed to evade further pain and humiliation.

Deep inside every adult lives a child – a child with its joys, fears, and memories. These memories become an integral part of one's personality, influencing our perception of ourselves and the world around us. Jim is an example of how childhood impressions can be defining in one's later life.

Delving into Jim's childhood, there are numerous instances where he felt rejected or misunderstood. Recall the day he first watched a baseball final. His admiration for the game was so intense that he was eager to share his feelings. However, the older neighborhood kids didn't notice him, and the boy stood on the sidelines, unable to muster the courage to join the conversation.

This moment became symbolic for Jim – a symbol of his invisibility and silent solitude. Many of us remember times when we yearned to be heard and understood, and every such instance leaves an indelible mark on the soul.

Over the years, Jim developed a particular reaction to failures. Rejections and setbacks made him withdraw even more, avoiding challenges and new opportunities.

The Secrets of Living

When he expressed a desire to play baseball, his father dismissed the idea, citing the costliness of training and Jim's lack of athletic talent. Such moments taught the boy that the world was full of disappointments, and it was better not to try to change anything.

Not only his parents, but also those around him often failed to see the potential in Jim. People reacted to him based on his behavior, a behavior ingrained in him by his parents and close ones. Peer ridicule, teachers' disbelief in his ability to learn, accusations for deeds he never did – all of this shaped Jim's worldview where he felt insignificant.

These instances became part of his identity. He grew accustomed to the idea that his opinions and feelings didn't matter, that he wasn't deserving of better.

College is a time of new opportunities, discoveries, and unfortunately, mistakes. For many, it's a formative period, the foundation for a successful future. But what do you do when you feel the world is against you? When you feel unreasonably outcast and create a context for such treatment? Jim faced a series of challenges in college, many of which, regrettably, he simply let pass.

Attending college became a real test for Jim. His attitude towards his studies was ambivalent: on one hand, it was an opportunity to prove to himself and others that he was capable of more, but on the other – there was the fear of failure, of being misunderstood or rejected again.

Jim frequently skipped classes and avoided extra efforts to rectify mistakes. This was his way of self-preservation from potential failures. It was better not to try than to face another defeat.

However, not everything was bleak. One of the college professors, seeing potential in Jim, tried to engage him in active academic life. He offered help, consultations, and closely monitored his progress. But Jim took this as an attempt to control him, or worse, as pity. Rejecting the help became yet another missed opportunity for personal growth.

College isn't just about academics; it's also about social life, interacting with peers, and participating in events. But Jim often avoided this. He found it hard to relate to his peers, as many of them saw him as a "loner." The lack of friends and a social circle intensified his feelings of isolation. He not only failed to create opportunities for himself but even managed to overlook and reject the ones presented to him.

Communication is a complex process, made even more complicated when it involves interactions between men and women. Stereotypes and barriers, created by past experiences or societal perceptions, can hinder mutual understanding.

At one college event, Jim met Linda. She was a vibrant, self-assured girl who effortlessly made new acquaintances (or at least wanted to appear that way, which essentially amounts to the same thing). In contrast to Jim, who often felt out of place, especially in the company of the opposite gender.

It seemed they had a great chance to get to know each other better. But when Linda, perhaps indirectly, invited him to spend time together, Jim saw this as a potential threat. His apprehensions, rooted in past experiences and fears, compelled him to react abruptly and leave, without even attempting to understand Linda's true intentions.

Deep-rooted reasons underlay Jim's behavior. In the past, he faced ridicule and belittlement from others, leading to his stereotype that people (especially girls) would only interact with him for amusement or to mock him. This idea became so deeply ingrained that even Linda's sincere desire to get to know him was perceived as a threat.

Society also plays a role in shaping our perceptions of ourselves and others. Stereotypes such as "strong man" or "weak woman" can heavily distort the real perception of a situation, creating additional barriers in communication.

Jim encountered several problems in communicating with the opposite gender due to his internal barriers and the influence of stereotypes.

Psychological Defense Mechanisms and Their Role in Jim's Behavior.

Each of us, to varying degrees, uses psychological defense mechanisms to cope with internal conflicts, fears, and anxieties. These mechanisms help us adapt to complex life circumstances. However, like any tool, they can be used both constructively and destructively. Let's consider this using Jim as an example.

Defense mechanisms employed by Jim:

1. Denial. One of Jim's primary defense mechanisms was denial. When he faced issues in his studies or social interactions, he often rejected their significance, claiming that "it's not for him" or "he's not interested".

2. Rationalization. Jim justified his failures with external circumstances or blamed others. For instance, he might say that the teachers simply don't understand him or that girls, like Linda, are just looking for a reason to laugh at him.

3. Regression. In challenging moments, Jim might revert to childlike behavior, seeking solace in things familiar and comfortable to him.

These defense mechanisms acted as temporary "safety cushions" for Jim. They allowed him to avoid direct confrontations with unpleasant emotions and feelings. For example, denial helped him avoid feeling like a failure, while rationalization allowed him to shift responsibility onto others.

However, the long-term use of these defense mechanisms came at a cost. Jim missed opportunities for personal growth and development. He often avoided reality, leading to deteriorating relationships with others and missing many chances in life.

Moreover, by avoiding confrontation with reality, Jim deprived himself of the chance to learn how to cope with difficulties and become more resilient to life's storms.

Psychological defense mechanisms play a crucial role in everyone's life. They help us deal with challenges, but they can also be the cause of many issues. Recognizing and controlling their use is key to a healthier and happier lifestyle.

Main psychological processes manifested in Jim's behavior:

1. Formation of defense mechanisms - instinctive reactions aimed at protecting the psyche from unpleasant emotions and memories.

2. Established low self-esteem - a distorted perception of one's abilities and potential, leading to the avoidance of challenges and new opportunities.

3. Social relationship issues - difficulties in interpreting social cues and an inability to build trustful relationships.

These processes, formed against the backdrop of past failures and difficulties, became the main obstacles to Jim's personal and social development.

CHAPTER TREE

Where Does Self-Confidence Come From?

There are moments in everyone's life when they face a choice: to fight or to give up. Moments when it feels like everything is against you, and the easiest thing is to just throw in the towel, accept the situation as it is, and not try to change anything. For Jim, such a moment came after a failed college experience when he felt lonely and unhappy.

After a series of academic failures and unsuccessful attempts to make friends, Jim felt lost. The feeling that he was unnecessary to anyone and that nothing good awaited him grew increasingly persistent. In such moments, people often seek solace in the past, recalling happier days and comparing them to the present.

Jim frequently revisited memories from his childhood when everything was much simpler. He dreamed of returning to that time when there weren't as many responsibilities, anxieties, and disappointments. But deep down, he knew it was impossible.

Many of his acquaintances, seeing his state, advised him to "just go with the flow". Some said it was just a "dark period" and things would change soon. But to Jim, these words sounded hollow.

Real life swiftly and harshly brought Jim back to the need to earn money.

The next morning started with an unexpected breakfast conversation. Jim's father looked at him with a somber expression. "You can't go on living like this. We need money, and you need to work," he said.

Jim was shocked. He had always felt he was too young to worry about things like a job. He dreamed of going back to college, trying again but in a different major, finding his path. But life put him in front of a fact: his family was in financial difficulty, and he couldn't stand aside.

Jim's mother tried to comfort him. "We just want you to understand responsibility," she said.

Jim spent the next few days job hunting. Without education and work experience, it wasn't easy for him. But thanks to his determination and desire to help his family, he got a job in a local store. Days went by in a blur: routine tasks, lunch breaks, and tired evenings.

Working at the store taught Jim a lot. He began to understand the value of money and learned to appreciate every cent he earned. Every day, he faced real problems that required immediate solutions. Jim learned to be responsible, disciplined, and persistent.

Even though working in the store was far from his dream (he didn't have a clear dream anyway), Jim realized that it was just a temporary challenge. He started saving money, dreaming of going back to school, getting an education, and pursuing his ambitions.

In his early days at the new job, Jim tried to minimize interactions with his colleagues. He didn't want to get attached to this place, considering it just a temporary stop on his way to his real life. But over time, driven by the human need for social interaction, he began to get to know his coworkers.

One of them, Henry, was about twenty years older than Jim. He had been working at the store for over a decade and was known as its "steady pillar." On one lunch break, when Henry and Jim happened to sit together, Henry began talking about how much he loved his job.

"Many people see this job as just a stepping stone," he began, "but for me, it's a dream. I've always wanted to work right here. This is my place, and I'm ready to work here until I'm old."

Jim was taken aback. He found it hard to believe that someone could dream of being a store clerk their whole life. He silently listened to Henry, trying to understand what makes someone limit their dreams to such a seemingly mundane and trivial goal.

Henry continued, "Here, I feel needed. I know all the regular customers, and they know me. This gives me a sense of stability and confidence in tomorrow."

Jim realized he didn't want that kind of life. His dreams were broader, his ambitions higher. He didn't want to settle for less and spend his whole life in one place, content with only the small joys.

This conversation gave Jim another push to never settle, to seek new opportunities, and aim higher. He understood that the course of his life was his choice, and only he decided the size of his dreams. As he worked more hours and spent more time outside his home, he began to communicate less with his parents. Strangely enough, he started reflecting on himself more often, considering his own desires. He noticed that he felt less depressed, now, he wasn't indebted. He was earning his money and wasn't obliged to unconditionally obey his parents' will.

One day, while taking a walk after work, he spotted an advertisement for a painting course. It was a chance to gain additional education and improve his skills. He was tired of wandering around the store without acquiring any valuable profession. Jim decided to seize this opportunity.

Which effective qualities can we identify for consideration that are on the surface, seemingly simple at first glance, but fundamental at the same time? What primarily determines our effectiveness, success, and happiness?

1. Decisiveness and self-confidence.

Ineffective: Indecisiveness, reliance on others' opinions, low self-esteem.

2. Proactivity.

Ineffective: Reactivity. People react to events instead of anticipating them and actively managing the situation. Reaction only occurs when the consequences of your ineffective actions have already manifested.

3. Ability to set and achieve goals.

Ineffective: A lack of clarity in goals or constantly postponing their realization.

4. Hard work, the ability to work diligently and persistently towards one's goals, even when it might be challenging or tiring. This quality allows people to overcome obstacles, stay motivated, and achieve their ambitions.

Ineffective:

Laziness. A lack of desire or motivation to perform any work or activity. Frequently avoiding effort or preferring minimal energy expenditure.

Indifference. A lack of interest or stimulus to act, apathy towards the results of one's actions or their absence.

Apathy. A detached or absent emotional state, manifested in a reluctance to do or change anything.

Passivity. A lack of initiative, preferring decisions to be made for oneself. Waiting for other people or circumstances to act instead.

5. Adaptability, flexibility in thinking.

Ineffective: Rigid perception, unwillingness to change or accept new information.

6. Emotional resilience and self-regulation.

Ineffective: Emotional instability, frequent mood swings, difficulties in managing one's emotions.

7. The ability to listen and understand others.

Ineffective: A lack of active listening skills, interrupting the interlocutor, an inability to understand another person's point of view.

8. Self-discipline and persistence.

Ineffective: Easily distracted, lack of discipline, procrastination.

To achieve success and happiness, many people can identify and correct ineffective behavior patterns. Here are some of them:

1. Low self-esteem.

How it forms: It may result from negative upbringing, childhood criticism, or past failures.

Correction: Work on strengthening self-esteem through self-reflection, acquiring useful skills, leading to a sense of possibilities instead of helplessness.

2. Lack of goals.

How it forms: It may be linked to self-doubt or fear of the future.

Correction: Identify your values and set clear, measurable goals.

3. Procrastination.

Procrastination is the act of delaying or postponing the execution of a task or a series of tasks, despite understanding the potential negative consequences of such delay. It's when a person, aware of the importance and necessity of completing a certain task, still puts it off in favor of less important or even irrelevant tasks.

How it forms: Procrastination can be caused by various factors such as fear of failure, self-doubt, perfectionism, lack of motivation, or simply a reluctance to do an unpleasant task.

Correction: Break tasks into smaller steps, use the Pomodoro technique, and create a clear schedule.

4. Perfectionism.

The pursuit of high-quality work and a responsible attitude towards tasks is generally a positive quality. However, if such a desire is driven by a fear of criticism, making mistakes, and subsequent condemnation by others, and leads to stress and frustration, then this destructive perfectionism becomes a problem. It hinders productivity or negatively affects a person's psychological well-being.

How it forms: It can arise from a fear of criticism or high self-imposed standards.

Correction: Acknowledge that mistakes are part of the learning process and set realistic standards.

5. Victim mentality.

How it forms: It stems from the habit of blaming external circumstances or other people for everything.

Correction: Work on taking responsibility for your life and your decisions.

6. Approval-seeking.

How it forms: It can develop from a need to be accepted or loved.

Correction: Recognize your uniqueness and value and learn to say «no."

7. Conflict avoidance.

How it forms: It may result from a fear of negative emotions or a reluctance to create problems.

Correction: Develop assertive communication skills and the ability to express your feelings and opinions.

Many of these ineffective behavior patterns are formed based on past experiences, interactions with others, or cultural and social expectations. Understanding the roots of the problem and working on its correction can significantly improve a person's quality of life.

It's a bitter realization, but many people primarily seek change only after experiencing significant declines in their quality of life. They often respond to changes in their lives only when they keenly feel discomfort or crisis. This can be associated with several psychological processes:

1. Comfort zone. We often strive to maintain the status quo and stay within our comfort zones. Until the level of discomfort reaches a certain critical point, many of us prefer not to change anything.

2. Pain avoidance. The human brain is wired to avoid pain and seek pleasure. As long as problems or difficulties do not cause noticeable pain or discomfort, people may ignore them or postpone dealing with them.

3. Fear of the unknown. Change involves uncertainty, and many people are afraid of the unknown. They may avoid changes until the current situation becomes unbearable.

4. Cognitive inertia. People tend to stick to their beliefs and habits, even if they are ineffective. This is a kind of "psychological inertia" that can slow down the process of change.

However, it's worth noting that not everyone reacts this way to crises or decline in their lives. Some individuals have a high level of self-awareness and proactivity, allowing them to make changes in their lives before encountering critical situations. And some people don't even react during acute crises, continuing to go with the flow.

After his conversation with Henry, Jim spent a considerable amount of time reflecting on his future and what he truly wants from life. This chance encounter became a catalyst for a reevaluation of his values and ambitions.

The conclusions Jim reached are as follows:

1. The Significance of Dreams. Jim realized that dreams should not be limited by one's environment or the opinions of others. They should be sincere and reflect an individual's true aspirations.

2. The Importance of Self-Development. By staying in one place and not striving for improvement, a person can miss out on many opportunities. Jim recognized that he needed to invest in his education and skills to open up new horizons.

3. Autonomy in Decision-Making. Others' experiences, even if they seem instructive, may not always be applicable to one's own life. Jim decided that he would be the captain of his own ship and chart his own course.

The goals Jim set for himself are as follows:

1. Education. Jim decided to return to school. He began searching for evening courses and online programs that would allow him to balance work and learning.

2. Social Connections. Understanding the importance of communication and relationship-building, Jim decided to dedicate more time to socializing, attending events, and expanding his circle of acquaintances.

3. Career Advancement. Jim did not want to remain in a low-paying and unfulfilling job for the rest of his life. He began seeking opportunities for professional growth, including internships, courses, and seminars in his field.

Jim realized that life is something greater than mere existence.

Where Does Confidence Come From?

Confidence is a state of believing in one's abilities, knowledge, and decisions. It can stem from various sources:

1. Experience. Past successes can reinforce a person's belief in their abilities. When we accomplish something and achieve success, it strengthens our sense of competence.

2. Preparation and Knowledge. Deep knowledge in a specific area or thorough preparation can enhance the feeling of confidence.

3. Positive Thinking. An optimistic outlook on life and self-belief can boost confidence even during challenging times.

4. Feedback. Positive feedback from others can elevate self-esteem and reinforce a sense of confidence.

5. Self-Acceptance. Accepting oneself as they are, including recognizing both strengths and weaknesses, contributes to the development of enduring self-confidence.

6. Comparison with Others. Sometimes people feel more confident when they compare themselves to others and realize that they are not inferior (although this source can be double-edged, as excessive comparison can also decrease confidence).

7. Continuous Practice. Regular engagement in an activity, skill improvement, and achieving results reaffirms the ability to accomplish tasks.

It's important to understand that confidence is not a static quality; it can change depending on circumstances, experiences, and personal growth. Some people may feel confident in one area of their life and less confident in another.

Imagine that you were fortunate enough to be born and raised in a supportive environment where you received guidance, were taught effective communication skills and self-confidence, had the opportunity to develop necessary skills, and were encouraged to persevere. You've felt self-realized from an early age, and self-confidence has always been a natural part of who you are.

No matter how life unfolds for such individuals, they often encounter fewer challenges compared to those who had fewer advantages.

The secret of people who achieve success in life is, to a large extent, a result of how they were raised. Consider the role of parents: active involvement in a child's life, mentorship, encouragement of diverse interests, and skill development. Think about the children who attended various clubs and activities—not only did they learn to play sports or paint but they also adapted to new social environments, learned to work in teams, and overcome obstacles.

Compare this approach with the "lessons of life" method, where a child is brought up on the streets or in conditions of limited adult supervision. Here, peer interactions play a significant role, but often without adult guidance.

Successful parents, typically from the middle class, often interact with their children through dialogue rather than issuing commands. They seek not just to impose their point of view but to discuss and analyze various aspects of a situation. This approach helps children develop critical thinking skills.

While low-income parents may avoid interacting with teachers or school administration due to fear or lack of confidence, middle-class parents actively engage in their child's school life. This creates an atmosphere of support and understanding.

As a result, children growing up in such an environment, having learned to overcome difficulties and not fearing to express their opinions, often feel more confident in society as they enter adulthood. They are unafraid of encountering challenges and know that persistence and adaptability will enable them to succeed in any situation.

Children from middle-class families exhibit noticeable confidence and initiative. They frequently express themselves in public settings where they feel free and comfortable. An example of such behavior might be discussing a new book with friends at a café, not hesitating to share their opinions and preferences. They not only actively share their knowledge but also expect to be listened to. For instance, middle-class children may easily ask additional questions of a teacher if something was unclear.

These children are well-informed about social norms and rules. By the time they reach the third grade, many of them have learned how to act in their favor, seeking help from authorities such as teachers or doctors to achieve their goals.

On the other hand, children from less privileged families often display restraint and caution. Their behavior can be described as reserved or cautious. They may not feel confident enough to voice their opinions or change a situation in their favor.

Besides psychological aspects, a person's confidence is greatly influenced by their personal skills in various areas. To feel more self-assured, it's important to be competent in various skills. So, how can you acquire skills if you weren't taught them in childhood?

Indeed, self-confidence often correlates with competence in specific areas. If a person possesses certain skills and knows they can successfully accomplish certain tasks, it automatically increases their self-confidence. However, if opportunities to acquire these skills were not provided in childhood, it doesn't mean that it's impossible for an adult to develop them.

1. Adult education. Nowadays, there are numerous resources for adult learning. Online courses, webinars, workshops, and other formats allow people to continue learning throughout their lives.

2. Reading and self-education. Libraries, bookstores, and internet resources offer countless materials on self-improvement and acquiring new skills.

3. Practice. Mastering a new skill requires practice. Start small, set yourself achievable goals, and gradually increase their complexity.

4. Support groups. Join communities or groups where people share your interests. Communication and sharing experiences with like-minded individuals can be an invaluable resource.

5. Mentoring. Find someone who possesses the skills you want to acquire and ask them to be your mentor. Learning under the guidance of an experienced specialist can be very effective.

In the end, despite initial gaps in education or skills, anyone can compensate for them by actively engaging in self-education and practice. Most importantly, each new skill or knowledge adds to confidence and enables individuals to feel more competent in various life situations.

A more successful and practical way to acquire a skill is by receiving some form of incentive. Don't hesitate to take up an internship in a field you wish to explore. Even if the pay might be modest, it will serve as an added motivation.

Immersing yourself in a real professional environment often proves to be the most effective method for gaining hands-on skills. As an intern, you're not just learning a new trade or skill; you're gaining invaluable real-world experience that theoretical training simply can't match. The knowledge you gain from books or lectures doesn't always align with real-world challenges. In practice, you might encounter situations you never even considered while studying theory. On the job, you'll have the opportunity to interact with seasoned colleagues who can offer valuable insights and demonstrate the right way to accomplish tasks. As an intern, you also build a network of professional contacts that may benefit you in the future. Even a modest stipend can be motivating; it's not just compensation for your effort but also an acknowledgment of your potential as a specialist.

Thus, an internship or an assistant's role in your field of interest can be the ideal solution for those wanting practical experience while also being financially incentivized. It also accelerates the learning process since you can immediately apply what you learn.

Furthermore, I'd like to share a list of skills that can be beneficial in daily life. Hobbies and passions are more than just ways to pass time. They are bridges to self-awareness, making you more profound, versatile, and valuable in various life facets.

1. Dancing. To dance is to communicate with your body. It's not just entertainment. Dancing teaches us the harmony of movement, training our flexibility and coordination. It improves your posture, instills confidence in your stride, and adds charisma. Both the dance floor and dance classes serve as excellent venues to meet individuals, potentially of the opposite gender.

2. Learning Foreign Languages. Our world is brimming with languages, each one being a key to a new culture. As you delve into a new language, you're broadening

your horizons, opening yourself up to international communication, and unveiling new career prospects.

3. Oratory Skills. Speaking both confidently and eloquently is not merely a gift but a skill. Once mastered, you can stand as a beacon of authority in any sphere, taking on leadership roles.

4. Culinary Arts. To cook is to create. Culinary arts blend science and creativity seamlessly. A dish crafted with expertise can be the star of any table, a true cause for pride. Moreover, it's an engaging profession.

5. Creativity and Crafts. Activities like painting, knitting, or handcrafting aren't just about self-expression. They teach patience, an appreciation for detail, and offer tranquil escape.

6. Sports Activities. Engaging in team exercises or competitions not only enhances physical condition but also builds camaraderie and nurtures new friendships.

7. Musical Instruments. Playing a musical instrument harnesses a wide range of cognitive and physical skills simultaneously. Beyond that, music has the power to weave hearts together, serving as a universal language for everyone.

8. Online Social Engagement. Being active in online conferences, webinars, and various instructional sessions offers a golden opportunity to widen your professional horizons and foster valuable social ties. For instance, through a marketing webinar you might meet leading specialists in that domain.

9. Diving into Psychology. Exploring the psychological aspects of human interactions can sharpen your perception of those around you and enable the establishment of harmonious relationships with a diverse range of individuals.

10. Shared Interests. Whether you join a book club or a community of rare plant enthusiasts, a shared passion strengthens social bonds and enriches your experiences.

11. Driving Skills. Mastering the art of driving offers you the freedom of movement. It's more than just a mode of rapid transit; it's the ability to embark on autonomous journeys where you chart the course. Moreover, driving hones your concentration and teaches responsibility.

12. Cultural Enrichment. By attending theaters, galleries, and museums, you immerse yourself in the realm of art, making you a more informed and captivating conversationalist.

13. Creative Endeavors. Engaging in a variety of creative projects allows you to unveil your potential, showcase unique talents, and establish your reputation in a specific domain.

14. Professional Education and Skill Enhancement. Advancing your professional training paves the way to becoming an expert in your field.

Every passion enriches our experience, bringing unique insights and broadening our social circles. Not only does it add vibrancy to your life, but it also enhances your appeal to others. Never hesitate to explore new horizons, for with every new pursuit, you unveil another facet of your identity.

The quest for self-improvement bolsters our confidence in our decisions, allows us to lead a vibrant and fulfilling life, and aids in finding harmony between our inner world and the external environment.

CHAPTER FOUR

Taking Destiny into Our Hands.

Subchapter One

Jim's Palette of Change.

Jim was walking past an old building with peeling paint when a vibrant sign caught his eye: "Painting Courses. Discover a World of Color!" His heart skipped a beat. The time spent working in a store had somehow clouded his life, making it dull and monotonous.

On a whim, Jim immediately signed up for the course. On the first day, he felt out of place. Around him were people of different ages; some had bright tattoos, others wore clothing with patterns – they all seemed so confident.

"Hey, I'm Steve. First time here?" a man with a red beard approached him.

"Yes, I'm Jim. I've never held a paintbrush before," admitted Jim, leaving out his past affair with graffiti.

"Don't worry, you'll be painting in no time!" Steve replied with a smile.

During the course, Jim not only learned painting skills but also realized the significance of teamwork. He discovered that when every team member contributes, the outcome can be more rewarding.

One day, when Jim was selecting a shade for a significant project, Steve suggested trying "sunlit yellow". Jim had his doubts but decided to give it a shot. The result was astounding - the wall painted in that hue seemed to revitalize the whole neighborhood.

The Secrets of Living

With newfound confidence, Jim decided to leave the store and join a painting crew. When he shared this decision with his parents, their reaction was mixed.

"Jim, why have you decided to leave? The store offers stability. Aren't you afraid of losing this job and not finding a new one?" exclaimed his mother.

"Son, are you sure this is the right move? Will the new crew accept you?" his father doubted.

"I want to give it a try," Jim replied.

On the day Jim decided to leave the store, his colleague and friend Henry looked at him in disbelief: "Jim, are you serious? Why have you decided this?"

Jim took a deep breath, trying to explain his decision, "Henry, I just feel like I need a change. I can't spend my entire life behind this store's counter."

That evening, Henry tried to convince Jim to come back, painting bleak pictures of a future without steady employment. But Jim was resolute.

After attending several interviews, Jim found a position with a painting crew. The job was entirely new to him. The dynamics in the crew were different from the store: it demanded teamwork, coordinated actions, and a creative approach.

Admittedly, the first few days were challenging. Jim found it hard to fit into a team where everyone had known each other for years. But his colleagues were patient with the newcomer. Rob, the crew's senior member, was particularly supportive, becoming a mentor to Jim.

"Do you see that wall?" Rob asked one day, pointing to a house they were about to paint. "Your job is to make it so passersby stop and say, 'Wow! Who did this?'". It sounded playful, but there was a degree of seriousness in his words.

Jim poured his heart into his work, and it wasn't long before his efforts were recognized. He was learning not just the technique of painting but also the art of communication, bridging gaps with his colleagues and clients.

Months later, when Jim bumped into Henry by chance, his friend was taken aback by the transformation. Jim looked both happy and fulfilled.

For Jim, as for many of us, the foundations of his behavior were shaped by his environment. The early years of his life were surrounded by circumstances that did little to foster his growth. His family home, school, and friends all presented their own unique challenges.

He often pondered why some people became successful while others, possessing the same qualities, seemed stuck. The answer became clear: one of the key factors was the environment. Successful people found themselves in nurturing circumstances that facilitated their growth.

"If I can't change my past," Jim resolved, "I can shape my future."

Joining the painting course, he felt a blend of excitement and determination. The initial classes unveiled a world of new opportunities and, equally, challenges. He discovered intricacies he had never before considered. But each new day, each new exercise, made him better.

Joining his first crew was a test not only of his painting skills but also his social ones. Each member of the crew was unique, each with their own backstory and experience. Jim learned to listen and share, to recognize the strengths and weaknesses of his colleagues, and to problem-solve collectively. There were initial misunderstandings, but with time, these barriers dwindled. After all, everything takes practice.

The Secrets of Living

With every new task, Jim felt he was ready for more. When he decided to change jobs, he began actively seeking opportunities. During one interview, he was offered a position on a painting crew. He knew this was a step forward. However, when his parents learned of his decision, their reaction was mixed. Doubts, fear of the unknown, and their genuine concern for their son were evident in their words.

Jim spent the night reflecting on his parents' words. He grappled with doubts, but deep down, he knew he had chosen the right path. He realized that sometimes we have to make choices that might not always be popular with others. But the most important thing is to believe in oneself and move forward, overcoming challenges and learning from mistakes.

So, Jim continued on his path into a new life, filled with challenges but also joys.

After personal success in the painting business, it became clear to Jim that the boundaries of art were not confined to walls and ceilings. He dreamt of deepening his understanding of the art world and transferring his skills to canvas. This sparked the idea of enrolling in drawing classes.

Making the shift from painting jobs to the art of drawing seemed like a huge leap. But his crew members, seeing his passion and determination, were thrilled with his decision. "You've always had an eye for finding beauty in the ordinary, Jim," one of them said. "This is your chance to show the world your vision!"

In the classes, Jim immersed himself in a world where every line and every shadow could tell a story. His classmates, many of whom were experienced artists, shared their expertise and taught him to see the world from a new perspective. Drawing opened the gates to a world of deep emotions, where every canvas became a reflection of the artist's soul.

Once after a lesson, brimming with enthusiasm, Jim decided to show his parents his initial sketches. He expected delight and support, but their response was entirely different. "Are you sure anyone would be interested in this, Jim? It might be a waste of time, artists usually train from childhood," his mother commented offhandedly. His father added, "New hobbies are good, but don't lose touch with reality. You seem so uplifted, so content now, but things can take a turn for the worse, even worse than before. Remember that."

Jim was taken aback by their words, even a bit stunned. However, he understood that drawing for him wasn't just a new hobby; it was a means of self-expression and self-discovery. He recognized that everyone faces a choice: whether to follow their inner voice and passions or to yield to the opinions of others. Moreover, he was certain he felt far better and happier than before. Oddly enough, his mood seemed to dip after interactions with his parents, regardless of whether he shared his joys or discussed challenges. It appeared as though they weren't as concerned with his hardships as much as they were about his joys.

Subchapter Two

Too Heavy to Bear.

Let's consider Jim from the perspective of him being fortunate. Not everyone gets the opportunity to try and change the course of their life. Not everyone has the willpower to act, even if they realize they're in a less than ideal situation.

Every morning when our alarm rings, we face a choice: to continue living the same old life or to step into the unknown, embracing change. However, often in the path towards a new life, there are psychological barriers that can become significant obstacles. Let's delve into them.

Fear of the Unknown.

As stated in ancient parables, fear is the ever-present shadow of humanity. This is especially true when venturing into uncharted territories. Do you remember the feeling on the first day of a new school or job? That moment when excitement and fear blend into one. Such is the nature of the human psyche: we fear what we don't know. The fear of the unknown is perhaps one of the most ancient and deeply ingrained fears of humanity. But what exactly is this "unknown"? It's the space beyond our experiences, realms we haven't explored yet, ideas we haven't grasped. And it's often this fear of the "unknown" that becomes the stumbling block on the path to personal growth and self-improvement.

On a biological level, fear serves a crucial role – to protect us from potential dangers. Our distant ancestors, when faced with an unfamiliar threat, would experience fear, prompting them to act – either to flee or to attack. Similarly, when they heard rustling at night, they had two choices: decide it's just the wind and ignore it or assume a predator is lurking and run. We are descendants of those who assumed it was a predator and, as a result, survived. This predisposition to presume danger is hardwired into us.

In today's world, the fear of the unknown often isn't associated with a real threat to our existence. Instead, it manifests in hesitations before making significant decisions, a reluctance to change careers, or to embark on a new venture. Take Alex, for instance, a successful lawyer who always dreamt of owning a restaurant. His fear of the unknown, stemming from potential business risks, kept him from realizing that dream for the longest time.

Anita, 32, had been an accountant for over a decade. She craved change, fresh experiences, and professional growth. She dreamt of relocating to a new city and switching jobs. But every time an opportunity presented itself, she would procrastinate. Her fear of the unfamiliar and potential challenges made her cling to her comfort zone.

On a psychological level, this fear of the unknown is linked to our inner beliefs and stereotypes. "What if I fail?" is a question many of us grapple with when faced with a new task or life change.

Jill, a mother of two, hesitated for a long time about returning to work after her maternity leave. The fear of the unknown, worries about how her colleagues might perceive her, and if she could balance work with childcare, held her back.

Overcoming the fear of the unknown starts with understanding its roots. Reflection, counseling, meditation—these tools can help discern what triggers this fear and how to navigate through it.

When Alex realized his fear was rooted in the dread of losing stability and facing failure, he began seeking ways to conquer it. Attending workshops, consulting with a business mentor, and gradually executing his project, he managed to turn his dream into reality.

Fear of the unknown is a natural sentiment that can act as both a barrier and a catalyst for growth. What's essential is the ability to recognize this fear, understand its origins, and use it as a tool for personal development. While challenging, this is a highly effective exercise. When we learn to channel our fear into positive energy, it propels our growth and goal achievement. Here are some strategies to employ fear for personal development:

1. Acknowledge and Accept Fear. First and foremost, recognize your fear. Avoiding or denying it only amplifies its grip on you. Try jotting down your fears or confiding in a trusted individual.

2. Analyze the Cause of Your Fear. Endeavor to trace the origins of your apprehensions. It could be past failures, fear of others' judgments, or simply the unknown.

3. Ask Yourself, "What's the Worst That Could Happen?" By assessing potential adverse outcomes and coming to terms with them, you'll often discover that your fears might not be as daunting as initially perceived.

4. Adopt Positive Thinking. Swap negative thoughts with affirmative affirmations. Instead of thinking, "I can't," assure yourself, "I'll give it a shot."

5. Set Small Goals. Breaking down a larger task or challenge into smaller, more manageable chunks can help you steadily overcome your fears and move forward with confidence.

6. Practice Confronting Your Fears. Engage in situations that induce fear. This might include interacting with strangers, speaking in public, or tackling a new challenge at work.

7. Embrace Relaxation Techniques. Meditation, breathing exercises, or yoga can reduce anxiety levels and help you focus on the present moment.

8. Seek Support. Friends, family, or a professional therapist can offer the backing and resources you need to tackle fear.

9. Acknowledge Your Achievements. Celebrate moments when you've overcome your fears. Recognizing your progress can bolster your drive to continue growing.

10. Use Fear as Motivation. Remember that the most thrilling opportunities for growth and development lie just outside your comfort zone.

When we master the art of turning our fears into strength, it becomes possible to reach heights that once seemed insurmountable. Every new venture, every hurdle crossed, fortifies us, making us wiser, more resilient, and experienced. The unknown always presents an opportunity for new discoveries and insights!

Internal and External Limitations.

Throughout life, everyone faces various limitations. These can be either external or internal, and they impact our decisions, actions, and perception of the world. Let's delve into how these limitations work and how they can be overcome.

Internal Limitations.

These are obstacles that we create for ourselves based on our beliefs, fears, and perceptions. Often, we are the ones setting our own boundaries. Thoughts like "It's too late for me to change," "I'm not talented," or "I lack the experience" – do these sound familiar? These are internal limitations that act as invisible walls, holding us back. Self-beliefs such as "I'm not worthy," "I'm incapable," or "This isn't for me" can stem from past experiences, upbringing, or interactions with others.

Fears – The fear of failure, fear of rejection, or fear of standing out often stops us from taking new steps.

Habits and routines – Repetitive actions and thoughts can solidify our comfort zone, making us less receptive to change.

External Limitations.

These are factors beyond our control that influence our opportunities and choices. We live in a society that often imposes its own standards and expectations on us. Sociocultural norms dictate how one "should" live, what activities to engage in, and what goals to set. Based on our gender, age, profession, or social status, specific actions or decisions might be expected of us. Deviating from these expectations can lead to misunderstandings and even judgment from others.

Material and Time Constraints – We might lack the necessary resources or time to implement certain plans.

Overcoming Limitations.

1. Awareness. To overcome a limitation, you must first recognize it. Ask yourself, "What is holding me back?"

2. Reflection. Constantly examining your inner beliefs and feelings can help you understand their reality and relevance to your current situation.

3. Seek Support. Interacting with people who have faced similar obstacles can offer new perspectives and solutions.

4. Develop a Plan. Determine the steps you can take to overcome each limitation.

5. Take Action. Start small, make minor steps toward your goal, regardless of the challenges.

Limitations are a part of our lives, but they can also be a catalyst for growth and development if we learn to perceive and overcome them properly. When faced with barriers and obstacles, the key is not to lose faith in oneself. Psychological barriers are meant to be overcome. It's the pathway to personal growth and self-improvement. By acknowledging our fears and limitations, we can work to overcome them, making our lives brighter and more fulfilling.

Remember that everyone is unique, and only they can decide the path they wish to follow. Regardless of fears, limitations, and the opinions of others, it's vital to listen to your heart and go where true happiness and harmony await.

Willpower as the Key Element to Initiate Change.

Willpower represents our ability to control our actions, emotions, and resist temptations. Think of it as the "muscle strength" of the mind, enabling us to act in line with our goals even when external forces try to push us astray.

Take Rita's story, for instance. While working in a prominent firm, she aspired to climb the corporate ladder. Yet, she often faced the temptation to cut her working hours short or leave early. But it was her determination and longing for success, bolstered by willpower, that kept her on track towards her objectives.

In contrast, Mason struggled with overeating. Every time he felt stressed, he'd seek solace in food. However, through honing his willpower, he learned to manage his emotions, gradually breaking away from this detrimental habit.

Ways to Enhance Willpower.

We all have those moments when we feel we've succumbed to temptation or couldn't resist making a decision that isn't beneficial in the long run. But as exemplified by individuals like Joan and Steve, willpower isn't a fixed trait. Instead, it can—and should—be cultivated and strengthened.

1. Visualization.

Joan had always been a gifted artist. However, life's demands often pushed her passion aside in favor of more "practical" pursuits. One day, she decided to visualize her dream: hosting her first solo exhibition. By picturing this event in detail, she gained additional motivation and willpower to practice and refine her art daily.

2. Setting Short-Term and Long-Term Goals.

Steve aimed to become a marathon runner. He knew he couldn't run 26 miles right off the bat. So, he began with shorter distances, setting increasingly challenging goals for himself. Each milestone achieved boosted his confidence and fortified his willpower for further training. Had he attempted the full marathon distance immediately, he likely would have fallen short.

3. Surround Yourself with Support.

When Joan embarked on her artistic career, her friends and family backed her at every step. This support network granted her the extra willpower to persist, even when criticisms and doubts began to erode her confidence.

4. Mindful Approach to Obstacles.

Steve encountered various injuries and setbacks on his quest. Rather than giving in, he viewed these hurdles as temporary challenges, not insurmountable barriers. His mindful approach to difficulties bolstered his drive to keep pushing forward.

5. Practice Gratitude.

Every day, Joan jotted down in her journal moments of gratitude that brought her joy or fulfillment. This ritual reminded her of her progress and amplified her determination to stay on course.

Willpower is an invaluable resource that can be fortified and nurtured. Through the experiences of Joan and Steve, we've seen how the right approach and consistent practice can transform this inner strength into a formidable tool for achieving one's objectives.

Indeed, willpower can play a pivotal role in achieving success and realizing personal aspirations. Let's highlight a few remarkable individuals who, through sheer determination and persistence, achieved outstanding feats:

1. J.K. Rowling - The author behind the Harry Potter series. Before becoming one of history's most successful writers, Rowling went through a phase where she was jobless, divorced, and raising her daughter solo. She continued to write, despite numerous rejections from publishers, until her book was accepted and skyrocketed as a global bestseller.

2. Thomas Edison - A renowned inventor who conducted thousands of experiments before successfully inventing the light bulb. Edison firmly believed that failures were merely stepping stones to success.

3. Oprah Winfrey - A media magnate and talk show host. She navigated through various hardships in her life, including poverty, discrimination, and traumatic childhood experiences. Her indomitable willpower helped her surmount these challenges, making her one of the world's most influential women.

4. Nelson Mandela - A South African revolutionary and politician. After spending 27 years in prison for fighting against apartheid, he not only got released but also became South Africa's first black president. His unwavering will and convictions led to global acclaim and a transformative shift in his country's history.

5. Mahatma Gandhi - The leader of the Indian national movement against British colonial rule. He advocated for non-violent resistance, and through his perseverance and belief, inspired millions to fight for freedom and rights without resorting to violence.

These individuals epitomize that willpower, tenacity, and self-belief can surmount any barrier. Each of them harbored a spark that propelled them forward, regardless of the odds they faced.

Strategies for Refining Behavioral Scripts.

Behavioral scripts are sets of automatic reactions and actions we develop throughout our lives in response to certain situations. These scripts often stem from our past experiences and beliefs. While they can serve us well, there are times when they result in inefficient or undesirable behaviors.

Analyzing Current Behavior and Determining its Effectiveness.

To refine behavioral patterns, the first step is always self-awareness. Why do we act in one way and not another? Does this behavior align with our goals, or does it hinder us? Let's dive deeper into this process:

1. Observation Journal:

Steve always felt he was a habitual procrastinator. To understand the cause, he started keeping a journal, recording his actions and emotions throughout the day. This gave him insights into his behavior, revealing that he often postponed tasks when feeling tired or stressed.

2. Feedback from Others:

Joan noticed frequent conflicts at work. She sought candid feedback from her colleagues about her behavior. Their insights made her realize she occasionally came off as too aggressive in conversations.

3. Benchmarking:

Sometimes, it's helpful to measure one's behavior against benchmarks or models. For instance, if you're working in a team and aim to be a more effective leader, observe successful leaders around you and analyze what makes them efficient.

4. Cause and Effect Analysis:

Every action has an underlying reason. By understanding the reasons behind your actions, you can better manage your behavior. For example, realizing that you often eat out of stress can lead you to seek healthier coping mechanisms.

5. Determine Effectiveness:

After scrutinizing your behavior, ask yourself, "Is this behavior helping me achieve my goals?". If the answer is "no", it's a sign that change is needed.

Analyzing current behavior is an opportunity to gain clarity on your strengths and weaknesses. With this newfound understanding, you can embark on a journey to refine your behavioral strategies, ensuring they're more aligned with your personal goals.

Applying Cognitive-Behavioral Therapy Techniques to Modify Undesirable Behaviors.

Life-long behavioral patterns can both enhance and detract from our overall well-being. So, how can we reshape those that lead to undesired outcomes?

Barney had a lifelong fear of heights. This fear was so profound that even climbing a small ladder would trigger a panic attack. Gwen, on the other hand, constantly sought approval from others. Her overwhelming need to please often stopped her from expressing her opinions and acting in her best interests.

Both turned to a specialist who recommended cognitive-behavioral therapy (CBT) techniques as a solution.

1. Identifying Negative Beliefs. Gwen realized her need for approval was rooted in the belief that her self-worth was tied to others' opinions. Barney recognized that his acrophobia (fear of heights) was linked to an underlying belief that every height is synonymous with falling.

2. Challenging and Testing the Reality of Beliefs. With the therapist's guidance, Barney began exposing himself to heights in controlled, safe situations, understanding that not all heights are perilous. Gwen worked on cultivating a belief that her self-worth isn't determined by others' perceptions.

3. Developing New Behavioral Strategies. Gwen learned to voice her opinions, even when they differed from the majority. Barney started practicing breathing exercises to manage his fear.

4. Gradual Integration of New Strategies into Daily Life. Both worked on embedding these new behavior strategies into their routines. Barney began taking walks in parks with gentle slopes, while Gwen participated in discussions where she could confidently share her perspective.

By employing CBT techniques, Barney and Gwen were able to transform their behavioral scripts and enhance their life quality. Their journey exemplifies how awareness, analysis, and modification of our behavioral responses can lead to significant life improvements.

The Power of Visual Training.

Our memories and experiences, anchored by emotions, shape our ability to foresee and analyze future situations. Let's delve into the world of visual training to understand how it can be the key to effective behavioral refinement.

Irene had always been responsible for organizing family trips. Before embarking on a journey, she meticulously studied maps and routes. Initially, she looked at the entire route from a bird's-eye view on the map, visualizing every turn and intersection. Then, Irene immersed herself deeper, imagining herself behind the wheel, feeling the road, anticipating every movement, and mentally modeling the main segments of the road and the respective turns she would need to make.

From a psychological standpoint, Irene employed visual training to create neural pathways in her brain. This allowed her to navigate the route with ease and speed. When she actually drove, her brain already "knew" the route, making her feel confident.

Such training isn't exclusive to car journeys. Visualization aids in any situation where one needs to anticipate potential outcomes and prepare accordingly. What might be stressful for one person becomes routine for another due to proper preparation and visualization.

Imagine every problem or task as a route. Your mission is to traverse it mentally first, acknowledging all the "traps" and obstacles. Thus, when faced with the actual situation, you're primed to act swiftly and effectively.

Individuals who have had successful experiences in dealing with stressful situations and have anchored them with positive emotions no longer view these situations as stress-inducing. If during their childhood they first observed how their parents tackled such situations, and later tackled them themselves under parental guidance, they established and reinforced strong neural connections. These situations might not have always turned out favorably, making them negative experiences, as has occurred with others. In essence, an action was taken (or not taken), followed by a reaction.

Let's work on a mental walkthrough of the actual route before overcoming it.

Future Visualization: Rewriting Behavior in Stressful Situations (and Beyond).

First, let's create a couple of emotional anchors. They will help us gradually train our bodies to experience more suitable emotions in challenging situations.

Positive Emotional Anchor: How to Establish It?

An emotional anchor is a unique combination of memories, sounds, images, sensations, or anything else that triggers a specific emotional response. A positive emotional anchor helps you quickly regain your desired emotional state. Let's go through the step-by-step process of setting up such an anchor:

1. Get Comfortable: Find a comfortable position, preferably lying down or sitting. It's essential to have a relaxed body. Focus on your breathing. Take deep breaths and let yourself relax more and more with each breath. Concentrate on the sensations in your body.

2. Choose a Moment: Recall a vivid moment in your life when you felt on top of the world, filled with joy, confidence, or any other positive emotion. While remembering, try to place yourself in a private, quiet space where nothing can distract you.

3. Dive into the Memory: Immerse yourself in this memory as if you are experiencing it right now. What do you see around you? What sounds do you hear? What do you feel?

4. Amplify the Feeling: Try to intensify this feeling by making the images more vivid, the sounds louder, and the sensations richer.

5. Set the Anchor: Once you feel the peak of this positive state, do something specific and easily repeatable. For example, pinch two fingers together or touch your wrist. The key is for this action to be quick and easily repeatable.

6. Test the Anchor: Wait for a few minutes, and then repeat your action (e.g., pinch your fingers). If done correctly, you should instantly feel a surge of the desired emotional state.

7. Repeat: The more you activate your anchor, the stronger the association between the action and the evoked feeling will become.

Now, let's explore how to use these anchors to modify your behavior in stressful situations or whenever you'd like to evoke specific emotions.

In addition, you can set multiple anchors for different positive emotions and use them as needed. This is a simple and effective way to instantly change your emotional state.

The visualization technique not only allows you to "relive" situations but also to "experience" them as you would like. It's not just about recalling positive moments from the past; it's about purposefully modeling the future, where stressful situations become mere stepping stones to success.

We can model how we would like to react and behave in situations that were previously challenging for us. It's essential to vividly imagine the situation you'd like to change. Try starting by viewing it as if you're an observer, as if a camera is recording the scene where we'll be editing our behavior. As you visualize, attempt to change your behavior to match what you want to demonstrate. Strive to make the mental image as detailed as possible, including the surroundings, people, your reactions, body language, phrases, and emotions.

Excellent. Now, if the first step is complete, let's move on to the second. Place yourself directly inside the scenario, visualizing it from a first-person perspective (as if you're behind the wheel of a car). At the moments when you want to experience positive emotions, activate the emotional anchor you established earlier.

Repeat the entire exercise several times to ensure you've worked through the situation accurately and that your emotional anchor is effective. This way, we're training the desired behavior and creating the likelihood that when you reproduce it in reality, you'll experience positive emotions instead of negative ones that might hinder you from displaying the desired behavior.

Next, try to behave as you've visualized, but this time in reality. It should be significantly easier since you've already practiced mentally. If you encounter negative emotions while attempting to replicate the desired behavior, activate your emotional anchors; this should help. Strive to practice this as often as possible, whenever an opportunity arises and a suitable situation presents itself, to reinforce your new behavior. With each repetition, the skill will become more ingrained, and the neural connections will grow stronger.

For example, here's how Stan prepared for challenging situations. He often faced conflicts in the workplace, and each time, he felt uncomfortable. Once, while preparing for an upcoming discussion on a complex project, Stan decided to visualize this meeting. He imagined all possible contentious points and then visualized himself calmly and confidently reacting to them. As a conclusion to this visualization, Stan rekindled the feeling of satisfaction he experienced after a successful day of fishing. This way, he "pre-lived" the conflict situation in advance, and during the actual meeting, he felt confident and composed.

Drew had been plagued by a fear of public speaking for years. However, before an important presentation, she decided to try a new approach. Drew visualized her performance: she pictured the room, the people, and the potential tough questions. Then, she visualized how confidently and articulately she responded to them, with her colleagues nodding in agreement with her opinions. At the end of the visualization, Drew "activated" the feeling of pride in herself, which she felt as a child when putting on "concerts" for her stuffed animals. She then rehearsed her presentation several times. The emotional anchor helped her navigate through the actual performance with confidence and grace.

The visualization technique allows us to "rehearse" complex situations in advance, instilling new, more effective reactions and behavioral patterns. It's a tool that not only helps us react to situations but also allows us to shape their outcomes in our favor.

Besides the jokes, the method of pre-visualization has been in use for thousands of years. Ancient Greek athletes practiced visualization before competitions. They imagined themselves overcoming their competitors, savoring the taste of victory, and hearing the applause of the audience. This practice helped them focus on a positive outcome. The power of visualization has been known to humanity since ancient times, and despite various cultural and temporal contexts, the principle of its application remains unchanged. Envisioning a desired outcome in the mind is a powerful tool that can be used to achieve any goal, whether it's physical excellence, spiritual development, or personal growth.

Its effect is colossal, especially when considering the amount of time invested—it can accelerate learning exponentially. I have a friend named Dan who used to be terribly shy about approaching women; he'd just lose his words.

Dan was the typical "nice guy." He had plenty of friends, was intelligent and fun to be around, but when it came to meeting women, his usual confidence seemed to vanish. His heart would race, and his hands would get sweaty. These moments were a real blow to his self-esteem.

The Secrets of Living

One day, I suggested he try visualization. Every evening before going to sleep, he visualized confidently approaching a woman, starting a conversation, and her responding with a smile. In these daydreams, he felt comfortable and relaxed.

To reinforce his visualizations, Dan started studying various materials on dating. He watched videos, read articles to learn how to start and maintain conversations effectively. He also wrote down a few opening lines on a piece of paper that he could use in real life.

But to make this process even more effective, Dan decided to incorporate positive emotional anchors. He remembered a moment from his childhood when he won a school competition. The feeling of pride and satisfaction he experienced then became his anchor. Each time he visualized a successful interaction, he simultaneously recalled holding that trophy.

After several weeks of practice, Dan felt ready to try out his new skills in real life. He went to a café and spotted a woman sitting alone at a table. Recalling his visualizations and summoning the feelings of childhood triumph, he confidently approached her and struck up a conversation.

Although the first encounter wasn't perfect, Dan felt much more self-assured than before. He realized that the power of visualization and using emotional anchors really worked. Now, he had a new goal - to refine his skills and continue growing.

Lisa dreamed of having her own car, but she was terrified of taking the driving test. She had heard from her friends how difficult parking was, how easy it was to get lost while changing lanes, and how stressful city driving could be. However, Lisa decided to approach this challenge consciously.

Every day, after her driving lessons, Lisa devoted time to visualization. She would get comfortable in her chair at home, close her eyes, and imagine herself getting behind the wheel. In her imagination, the road was clear, the car obedient, and her hands confidently held the steering wheel. She mentally went through the exam route, feeling calm and confident. Parking between cars, changing lanes on the highway, driving in urban conditions - she visualized each step in great detail, repeating it several times.

To reinforce positive emotions, Lisa used an emotional anchor. She had adored riding carousels as a child and had always felt excitement and joy. Now, during her visualizations, she imagined that carousel, allowing these positive emotions to fill her. This anchor helped her maintain self-assurance while driving.

The results didn't take long to show. Within a week, her instructor noticed significant improvements in her skills. And when the day of the driving test arrived, Lisa passed it on her first attempt, leaving her friends in disbelief. They couldn't understand how she had mastered it so quickly. But for Lisa, the answer was obvious: the power of visualization and positive emotional anchors had done their job.

The Power of Learning and Self-Education in Shaping Behavioral Strategies.

James and Rita had always been close friends, sharing not just good moments but also their individual life challenges. James often found himself panicking in stressful situations, while Rita would avoid conflicts even when they were vital to address. Both knew these behavioral patterns held them back, but how could they tackle them?

This shared challenge led them to delve into the world of psychology, highlighting the pivotal role of learning and self-education in forging new behavioral strategies.

James took the first step by attending stress management workshops. It was there he learned about the brain's plasticity, its ability to rewire and forge new neural connections based on experiences. This revelation was a beacon of hope. Through meditation and visualization exercises, he imagined himself staying calm amidst challenging situations. Over time, his behavioral script transformed, turning him into a more confident and composed individual.

Rita, on the other hand, delved into books on assertive communication. She unearthed the idea that conflicts aren't inherently negative and can sometimes pave the way for constructive outcomes. By applying these new communication strategies, she transitioned from being passive to assertive.

Self-education became their secret weapon. They realized that to truly change behavior, one must understand its underlying mechanisms and consciously work on personal shortcomings. Learning equipped them with the tools to do so effectively.

Both James and Rita managed to surmount their behavioral hurdles, becoming more accomplished and happier individuals. Their journey underscored a vital lesson: re-evaluating behavior and proactive self-education are the cornerstones of personal growth and development.

Rewriting Your Life's Script.

Modern psychology posits that our behavioral scripts aren't set in stone. They can be adjusted and reshaped. Regardless of our age or the length of time we've adhered to certain life patterns, we always possess the capability to opt for change.

Life isn't just a series of events; it's a narrative that we author. If there are chapters in this story that displease us, we hold the pen to rewrite them. After all, each individual is the protagonist of their own tale and dictates the direction of the ensuing chapters.

The crux of this understanding is that everyone harbors the potential for transformation, for a more intentional and joyful life trajectory.

Don't linger for the perfect moment or external nudges. Start small, set tangible goals, and march towards them. Understand that self-improvement is a journey, not a final destination. Along this route, you'll not only acquire new skills and beliefs but also gain a profounder understanding of your own self.

Embrace mistakes and setbacks; they're the architects of our resilience and wisdom. Your life is your narrative, and you alone decide the theme of the next chapter.

CHAPTER FIVE

Practical Intelligence and the Tipping Point Effect.

Jim had always felt uneasy around strangers. However, recent months had marked a significant transformation in his life. Working in a painting crew and continuously interacting with colleagues of diverse ages and interests had made him more outgoing. Attending art classes, he not only sought to translate his feelings onto canvas but also grapple with his internal fears. He aimed to be receptive to new experiences, and most importantly, learn to interact with those around him.

During one of these sessions, his attention was captivated by a young woman with a discerning gaze and vibrant curls. Her name was Rachel. She seemed to be a newcomer to the group, but her confident strokes and unique vision of the world immediately drew Jim's admiration.

During a short break, summoning all his courage, Jim approached Rachel to discuss how she managed to depict characters on her paintings so vividly. Their conversation flowed effortlessly, and Jim was taken aback by how easily he connected with her.

"You know, I've always believed that humor is the best way to express oneself on canvas," Rachel shared.

Jim responded with a smirk, "Well, I've got a lot to learn then, because my paintings currently look more like humorless comic strips!"

Both of them laughed heartily, and the conversation took on a more animated turn. By the end, Rachel mentioned, "Hey, I'm hosting a dinner for a few friends this Friday. You should come, it'll be fun!"

With a newfound confidence Jim hadn't recognized in himself before, he replied, "I'd love to! And maybe after class, I can walk you home, if that's alright?"

Rachel smiled, "That'd be lovely."

As night descended upon the city after their art class, the urban air grew cooler, and streets shimmered with bright lights.

"You know, I never thought I'd muster the courage to attend these classes," Jim began, casting a slightly uncertain glance towards Rachel.

She smiled back, "Me too. But sometimes you need a change in life, don't you think?"

As they walked down the street, their elbows occasionally brushing against each other, the streetlights illuminated Rachel's face, revealing calmness and confidence. She began sharing stories from her childhood, about how her grandmother taught her to draw, and when she first realized that art was her passion.

Jim reciprocated with tales of his youth, about how he had once dreamed, or perhaps merely thought, of becoming a comic book artist. This whimsical ambition made him smile, immersing him in various imagined comic book plots. But then life had taken a different turn. "I've always found it hard to express my feelings," he admitted, "but with drawing... it's somewhat easier."

Their path took them past cozy cafes, vintage bookstores, and quaint parks. Unexpectedly, Rachel took Jim's hand and led him to a small garden square. A pond stretched out before them, reflecting the city lights. "I love it here. It's so peaceful," she whispered.

After a while of basking in the serenity and the view, Jim suggested they move on. Outside Rachel's home, he paused, gathering his courage, and finally admitted, "Rachel, I'm glad we met. Tonight... it's special."

She nodded, "It is for me too, Jim. Thanks for walking me home."

With that, she touched his hand and headed inside. Jim stood there, watching her go, knowing indeed that the evening was something extraordinary.

Friday came quickly, and Jim eagerly anticipated his dinner with Rachel. When he arrived at the restaurant, she was already there, accompanied by three of her friends. Jim felt a twinge of nervousness but remembered his recent breakthrough at the art class and decided he wouldn't let his shyness prevail.

"Jim, allow me to introduce: this is Emily, Thomas, and Louisa," Rachel said, pointing to each in turn. They all smiled, extending their hands in greeting.

Throughout dinner, Rachel skillfully steered the conversation, creating a relaxed and friendly ambiance. Emily turned out to be an art enthusiast, Thomas worked at a bookstore, and Louisa was an educator. Jim found common ground with each of them, sharing his passion for drawing and tales from his classes.

During the meal, Thomas inquired, "Jim, what made you decide to take up drawing classes?" The question paved the way for a deep and genuine conversation about dreams, fears, and desires of everyone present. Rachel listened with delight as Jim opened up about his experiences and beamed with pride when he talked about his quest for self-improvement.

As dinner drew to a close and conversations around the table became more casual, Louisa suddenly suggested, "Hey guys, how about we hit the dance floor tomorrow night? There's a new dance club opening in town, and I think it'd be fantastic!"

Rachel immediately lit up, "Oh, I've always wanted to dance! Jim, what do you think?"

Jim felt his heart race. Despite his achievements in communication and his newfound confidence, the dance floor was an area where he felt vulnerable. To put it mildly, he had two left feet. However, looking into Rachel's eyes, he knew he couldn't decline. "Why not? Sounds like a blast!" he replied with a smile.

As the dinner party wrapped up and everyone was leaving, Louisa approached Jim, "You're an amazing person, Jim. Rachel is lucky to have a friend like you." Jim smiled back, thanking her for her kind words.

On their way home, Rachel and Jim walked side by side, holding hands. Blushing, Jim confessed, "To be honest, I'm not much of a dancer." Rachel smiled gently, "That's alright. I'm not too picky. Thank you for coming tonight. It was a wonderful evening."

Jim nodded, "I'm glad you invited me. It was one of the best nights of my life."

After dropping Rachel off and making his way back, Jim's thoughts turned to the upcoming evening. The idea of possibly looking silly or out of place on the dance floor, especially next to Rachel, was nagging at him. But recalling his recent triumphs and challenges he overcame, he believed he'd figure something out.

The solution came unexpectedly. During a Saturday morning huddle – a regular planning session orchestrated by their team lead – Jim shared his dilemma with colleagues. One of them smiled, gave him an encouraging pat on the shoulder, and said, "You know, Jim, I had the same problem once. But I found a solution. There's crash course in dancing at 'Rhythm Studio'. I took it once, and after a few sessions, felt confident enough to hold my own on the dance floor."

Jim's eyes lit up, "Do you think they could help me?"

Michael nodded, "They specialize in helping folks like us master basic dance moves and gain confidence. You'll absolutely love it."

With gratitude in his eyes, Jim shook his hand. He decided he'd give the course a try. After all, he had nothing to lose, and the opportunity to have an unforgettable time with Rachel was worth any effort.

Without wasting a moment, Jim rushed to "Rhythm Studio". Fortunately, there was an available instructor willing to give him a lesson. For three hours straight, the instructor guided him through basic steps and movements. Knowing he wouldn't become a pro in such a short time, Jim was determined to at least grasp a few foundational moves.

That evening, as Jim and Rachel arrived at the club, he felt far more confident. Despite his imperfect moves and occasional missteps, he learned to relax and enjoy the process.

Louisa and Thomas were enthralled by the energy and passion with which Jim and Rachel moved on the dance floor. Even though Jim was far from professional, his newfound confidence and willingness to take risks allowed him to relish every moment of the night.

After a couple of lively and spirited dances, Jim and Rachel decided to take a breather at the bar. They ordered refreshing cocktails and picked up the conversation that began over dinner. The music playing in the background set a unique mood — subdued yet sensual.

Rachel talked about her childhood, sharing her passion for dancing, something she inherited from her mother. Jim, in turn, became increasingly candid, discussing his adventures, dreams, and hopes. Their eyes sparkled, their gazes intertwining in a magical dance of their own.

The last song of the evening began. A soft, romantic track that many couples used to wind down after the faster rhythms. With a shared glance, Jim and Rachel wordlessly made their way to the dance floor.

Jim took Rachel by the waist, and she draped her arms around his neck. Their bodies began to move slowly, swaying in rhythm to the music. Their faces drew closer, their breaths mingling, hearts beating in sync.

And then it happened.

Their lips met in a long-awaited, tender kiss. The moment felt like an eternity and yet, fleeting. Everything around them faded away: the music, the people, the lights. In that instant, it was just the two of them.

When the music quieted and their kiss ended, Jim and Rachel remained standing on the dance floor, immersed in their feelings and emotions.

"You're incredible! Thank you for dancing with me tonight," whispered Rachel.

Jim smiled in reply, "There's a lot I'd do for you."

Pasipovsky's First Steps at the Fair.

The sunny early summer morning granted a special mood to all the townspeople. The fair always was a place where colors, sounds, and scents blended together. Under colorful umbrellas, traders showcased their goods, each trying to attract the attention of buyers.

That morning brought a mix of excitement and novelty to Pasipovsky, a student from one of the city's schools. His academic performance had been less than stellar, and the vibrant fair always beckoned with its diversity and ambiance. The decision by his parents to send Pasipovsky to trade at the fair over the weekend was abrupt but made sense. "You'll work if you don't want to study," they believed.

For the first time, amidst this bustling life, Pasipovsky found himself as a seller rather than a buyer. He came to the fair with a dream of becoming a successful trader, but reality proved more challenging than he had anticipated. His booth was small and modest, and the first few hours went by without a single buyer.

Looking at his products, he pondered, "Why isn't anyone approaching? What am I doing wrong?" He noticed that a nearby vendor was actively engaging with customers, sharing stories about each product, highlighting their uniqueness. Meanwhile, another merchant used bright signage and showcased product demonstrations.

Observing these successful vendors, he sought to understand their secrets. During a lunch break, an experienced seller, noticing his confusion, approached him and shared his wisdom: "You know, the essence of selling is the ability to connect with your customers. You need to immerse them in your world, showing them that you have what they're searching for."

He took these words to heart. He began actively interacting with passersby, talking about his items, persuading them, and showcasing the benefits of his merchandise. By the end of the day, he had sold more than he had anticipated.

His school years hadn't been straightforward. Energetic and sociable, he had the knack for bonding with peers, orchestrating games, and creating a fun atmosphere. In class, he was always the center of attention when it came to entertainment. However, when it was about academics, his performance was lackluster. While others meticulously took notes from the board, he might be found doodling in his notebook or daydreaming of adventures.

Yet, that day at the market was a turning point for him. By the end of it, counting his earnings, he realized that for the first time in his life, he had achieved something meaningful. It wasn't just about the money – it was the embodiment of his efforts, his ability to communicate and persuade.

Returning home, he reflected on the day. He understood that success in life isn't just about knowledge and grades. It's about recognizing opportunities, adapting to circumstances, seeking solutions, and leveraging one's strengths.

The profit from the market not only brought him money but also self-confidence. Suddenly, it became clear that school grades were just one facet of life. True success depends on the ability to carve out one's path, taking into account individual strengths and talents.

That evening, as Pasipovski settled into bed, he felt a unique sense of happiness. He had finally found his calling, and he was determined to pursue it.

By dawn the next day, Pasipovski was already up and about. His parents were surprised; they usually had to spend quite some time nudging him awake in the mornings. The previous day's success had not only boosted his confidence but also ignited a burning desire to try again. Before leaving, he paid attention to every detail: he neatly packed all the goods into his basket, counted the change, and even took a few new items with him.

Arriving at the market, he chose a new spot, close to where many traders gathered. Pasipovski remembered how he had watched and learned from them the day before and decided to put some of those lessons into practice.

Soon, the first customers began to inquire about his goods. He not only spoke about the quality of the products but also intertwined little stories or intriguing facts into his pitch. This caught the customers' attention, and they soon began to linger around his stall for longer periods.

By day's end, Pasipovski once again tasted the sweet success. His merchandise was nearly sold out, and his pockets were heavy with coins. On his way home, he pondered his future. School assignments and lessons seemed trivial compared to the tangible opportunity to achieve real-world success.

That weekend flew by in a blink. Each day at the market was a new challenge and new victory for him. Deep down, Pasipovski was already daydreaming about the holidays. He envisioned fully immersing himself in trading, expanding his product range, and perhaps even recruiting a couple of friends to help.

As summer vacation commenced, Pasipovsky dove headfirst into the world of commerce. Assisting him were two of his friends. They were astounded by Pasipovsky's knack for creating such a flourishing venture and were keen to join his enterprise.

Day in and day out, the trio manned their stall at the marketplace. Their inventory diversified, spanning from food items to household knick-knacks. Pasipovsky prioritized product quality and presentation. He knew that fresh apples or attractively wrapped gifts would entice more customers.

One day, recognizing the need for mobility, Pasipovsky, having recently secured a driving license, purchased a used truck. This vehicle marked a significant turning point for his budding business. Now, he could transport a larger inventory, reach distant fairs, and even procure goods from wholesale outlets.

With each passing day, the business flourished, not just monetarily but also in bolstering Pasipovsky's self-confidence. Despite his mediocre school performance, he became a beacon of wisdom and guidance for his friends.

By fall, as the holidays neared their end and the frequency of fairs dwindled, Pasipovsky decided to tally up his summer earnings. Sitting in his room, he laid out all his transaction records and receipts. His old school notebooks, once filled with lessons, were now brimming with figures and calculations.

Flipping through the pages, he began to compute his profits. And when he arrived at the final tally, he was almost in disbelief. He had amassed an amount rivaling his parents' annual income!

This victory further cemented his self-belief. Pasipovsky realized he'd discovered his true calling. The education school provided, it seemed, was no longer pertinent to him. He quickly grasped that real-world applications often diverged from theoretical teachings. Yes, knowledge matters, but the art of communication, seizing opportunities, and embracing risks were the real determinants of his success.

Pasipovsky's final school year felt like a blur. His mind was preoccupied with plans for the upcoming trading season, fresh ideas, and strategies. Teachers noticed his absent-mindedness and lack of enthusiasm towards his studies. But to Pasipovsky, the school curriculum paled in significance to the lessons he'd learned about real life.

On a warm evening, as the Pasipovsky family gathered for dinner, the young man mustered the courage to address his parents. Determination and a hint of anxiety were evident on his face.

"Mom, Dad," he began, "I've decided not to go to college after school."

A stunned silence filled the room. The parents exchanged surprised glances. "Are you serious? A college degree is crucial for your future," his mother uttered slowly.

The Secrets of Living

"I understand your concerns," Pasipovsky continued, "but I've found my calling. Trading at the fairs hasn't just earned me money but clarified what I want from life. Besides, I've never excelled academically. I believe other skills might serve me better."

"But it's just a summer fling! You can't jeopardize your future over a fleeting interest," his father retorted, a hint of worry in his tone.

Undeterred, Pasipovsky opened his ledger, presenting his parents with his calculations. "Look at this," he asserted. "Last summer alone, I earned what many make in a year. And this is just the beginning. I have plans to expand and further increase profits."

After studying the numbers intently, his parents finally looked up. His mother's gaze softened. "We've always wanted the best for you - a solid education and a stable future," she began. "But if you truly believe in this path and are committed to working hard, we'll stand by you."

Meeting their gaze with gratitude, Pasipovsky heaved a sigh of relief. The conversation had been a real test for him, but now, with the endorsement of the people closest to him, he felt emboldened to forge ahead on his chosen path.

Pasipovsky continually expanded his ventures at the fairs. His truck was always filled to the brim with goods, and his stall attracted an ever-growing number of visitors at every event. However, he recognized that to truly evolve his business, he had to dive deeper into its intricacies.

With determination, he established a personal mini-library, curating books on economics, business management, and trading. Pasipovsky was nothing if not practical. He focused on chapters and sections that directly benefited him, eager to grasp the intricacies of market dynamics to better predict trends and refine his business strategies.

One day, while skimming through a financial magazine, he stumbled upon an article about stock trading. The concept of buying and selling shares, and the potential to invest in burgeoning companies, piqued his curiosity. He pondered, "Could I possibly apply my skills at such a sophisticated level?"

With each passing day, his fascination with the stock market grew. Pasipovsky started attending seminars, participating in workshops, delving into the fundamentals of market analysis, and acquainting himself with stock behaviors and the impact of various economic factors.

He recognized that stock trading was a realm in itself, where his market stall experiences might not directly translate. Yet, his insatiable quest for knowledge, his hunger for success, and his adaptability hinted that this could be the next chapter in his business journey.

"If I've succeeded at the fairs, why not test my mettle in the stock market?" he thought resolutely.

Five whirlwind years transformed Pasipovsky from a young man haggling at local fairs to a confident investor and trader on the stock exchange.

His initial phase in the stock market was daunting, with its rapid trading rhythms, fluctuating prices, and the pressing need for split-second decisions. However, his fairground trading experiences proved invaluable. It was his knack for sensing market vibes and adapting to shifting circumstances that cemented his footing in this new arena.

At first, Pasipovsky operated solo, analyzing the market and making trades on his own. However, as time went on, he realized that to truly grow and expand his endeavors, he needed a team. The first members to join him were two of his friends from his fair-trading days. Their insights and market perspectives enriched Pasipovsky's strategy.

As time progressed, the team expanded, encompassing professional analysts, traders, and economists. Under Pasipovsky's leadership, they crafted strategies, forecasted market movements, and researched companies whose stocks held promising investment potential.

Pasipovsky carved out his niche not just due to his successful trades but also because of his unique approach to business. His team functioned like a well-oiled machine, where each member understood their role and value.

Of course, there were setbacks, moments when Pasipovsky's decisions missed the mark. Yet, due to the team's cohesive spirit and collective effort, they always navigated through challenges, learned from their mistakes, and moved forward with renewed vigor.

Over those five years, Pasipovsky not only solidified his position in the stock market but also demonstrated that even without formal academic training, sheer determination, a thirst for learning, and belief in oneself can pave the way to success in any field.

Practical Intelligence.

Practical intelligence typically refers to an individual's ability to adapt to the world around them, solve everyday problems, and effectively interact within their social environment. While traditional intelligence tests measure logical and analytical thinking, practical intelligence is more associated with "common sense" and the ability to navigate real-life situations successfully. To develop practical intelligence, it's beneficial to have role models to emulate and the right environmental conditions.

Tipping Point Effect.

This term describes a moment or point where a minor change in external conditions or stimulus results in a significant, abrupt shift in the state or structure of a system. In sociology, for example, this could relate to the point where a critical mass of individuals supports an innovation, after which the innovation begins to spread exponentially within society. In psychology, a similar principle might describe the moment when accumulated experience or learning reaches a "tipping point," causing an individual to perceive or respond to information differently.

Both these concepts are central in various theories and studies within sociology and psychology, helping to shed light on the dynamics of human behavior and social processes.

In a way, there's no need to have an in-depth understanding of a specific subject or to be a complete professional in a particular skill. It's usually enough to have a solid foundational level in a set of essential knowledge and skills. Then, you can comfortably tackle any required tasks.

Imagine having ten keys, and only one of them opens the door you need. You don't necessarily have to know the intricate details of each key. Understanding which keys might fit the door and how to use them is sufficient.

The world around us is brimming with diverse success stories, each imparting crucial life lessons. One such tale is the journey of Pasipovsky, a man who truly understood the essence of practical intelligence, perhaps more than anyone else.

Many recognize Pasipovsky as a successful stockbroker, the leader of a sizable team. Yet, few are acquainted with his humble beginnings. School years for Pasipovsky weren't marked by top grades but by navigating through fairs and markets, where every sale was a mini-exam. It was in these bustling arenas that he mastered the art of communication and learned to perceive people's needs.

While the theoretical knowledge of Pasipovsky's peers might have been beneficial, it was his hands-on experience that proved invaluable. He knew how to apply his knowledge. Pasipovsky epitomizes the importance of practical intelligence—the ability to adapt to ever-changing circumstances and to devise solutions on the fly.

His stock market triumphs undoubtedly point to a tipping point in his career. It's that pivotal juncture when accumulated skills and knowledge reach a critical mass, propelling an individual to a new echelon of expertise and action.

However, it's worth noting that his journey also illustrates the survivorship bias. We hail him as a success, but many of his peers, who treaded similar paths, might not have scaled the same heights. This serves as a reminder that behind every success story, there's a myriad of failures and missed opportunities. Yet, it was Pasipovsky's sheer determination, self-belief, and ability to learn from his mistakes that have shaped him into the man he is today.

From this perspective, Jim didn't need to be a professional dancer; a basic set of skills sufficed. While he might not have been the star of the dance floor, he moved confidently, felt the rhythm, and most importantly, enjoyed himself. Rachel genuinely cherished every moment they spent together.

I'm not implying by the above that there's no need to be a professional. Far from it. Everyone should excel in their field, achieved through repeated practice and refinement. And it's more rewarding when you are motivated and reap benefits from honing a skill. However, there are numerous skills useful in life that aren't pivotal, and one can possess them at a foundational level.

Had Jim been completely unable to dance, that magical evening would have been lost.

So, what socially useful skills might come in handy and are worth mastering at least at a basic level? Which abilities will help you feel comfortable in almost any situation? Let's delve in.

Social skills, even when grasped at a rudimentary level, can significantly enhance the quality of your relationships. They assist in adapting successfully across diverse sociocultural situations, making life much more comfortable. Here are some of them:

1. Communication Skills. The ability to listen actively, pose the right questions and engage in a dispute-free conversation.

2. Empathy. Understanding and acknowledging others' feelings and the ability to put oneself in their shoes.

3. Conflict Resolution. Recognizing the root causes of disputes and seeking efficient ways to resolve them.

4. The Art of Saying "No". Protecting your boundaries without infringing upon others'.

5. **Driving:** Allows for mobility, convenient trip planning, and reduced dependence on public transportation.

6. Basic First Aid. In critical situations, knowing how to provide first aid can save a life.

7. Dancing Skills. Helps boost confidence at festive events and social gatherings.

8. Building Rapport. The knack for quickly establishing friendly or professional relationships.

9. Etiquette. Understanding the basic norms and rules of communication across various cultures and environments.

10. Basic Cooking. Being able to prepare a few good dishes can come in handy when hosting guests or trying to impress loved ones.

11. Foreign Language Knowledge. Even basic proficiency can assist during travels or when interacting with foreigners.

12. Self-presentation. The ability to put oneself in the best light, showcasing strengths and skills.

13. Basic Self-defense, Swimming, and Fitness. Essential for personal safety, recreational activities, and maintaining good health.

14. Stress Management. Various relaxation techniques and methods for managing tension.

15. Teamwork. Understanding one's role and contributions to a collective project or task.

16. Critical Thinking. The skill to analyze information, identify key points, and make logical conclusions.

17. Photography Basics. Useful for capturing quality photos during travels, at family events, or for social media.

18. Event Planning Basics. Useful for organizing events, be it a corporate function or a birthday party.

19. Basic Gardening or Botany. Helpful for caring for plants at home or a summer house, and can also serve as a wonderful hobby.

20. Basic Repair and Handicrafts. Being able to mend or create something with your own hands can be both practical and economical.

Mastering even the foundational principles of these skills can help you navigate most social situations with increased confidence and ease.

The process of self-improvement is an endless journey where one discovers new horizons and opportunities. Every new day brings fresh lessons, challenges, and revelations. Understanding that our potential is limitless and that we can always become a better version of ourselves drives us forward, spurs our growth, and inspires us to discover new avenues for self-fulfillment. The realization that achieving a goal is feasible in the near term provides the impetus to start learning new skills.

Life is a dynamic process, and by constantly moving forward, we leave our mark, making the world a slightly better place and becoming a source of inspiration for others. After all, the pursuit of perfection is about the journey, not the destination.

CHAPTER SIX

The Magic Mirror: Who's Beside Us.

Jim confidently placed the last element of the dinner on the table – a freshly made salad. Today was the day he had finally decided to share the news about Rachel with his parents.

"So, how was your day?" Jim began, trying to lighten the atmosphere.

"Just another day, son. How about yours?" replied his mother, smiling.

"Not too bad, not too bad..." Jim trailed off, picking up his fork and beginning to eat. "By the way, I have some news. I'm seeing Rachel."

His mother put down her fork, and his father looked at him with a stern expression.

"Rachel?" his mother enquired slowly, "Isn't she the girl you introduced to us recently when we were at the park?"

Jim nodded.

"Yes, that's her. We've been dating for a couple of months now."

"Son, are you sure this is a good idea? She seemed a bit headstrong to me," his mother remarked.

"Not just headstrong," his father chimed in, "Her family has its issues, you know."

Jim felt his initial enthusiasm wane, replaced by irritation and a sense of being misunderstood.

"I know you're concerned, but..." Jim began.

"Son," his father interrupted, "we just want you to be happy. And happiness in relationships can be complicated. There's a lot you might not have considered."

"That's precisely why I want to figure it out on my own," Jim responded firmly.

A silence ensued. Looking at his parents, Jim understood that their apprehensions stemmed from concern. Yet, he couldn't let that concern hold him back.

"I understand your worries. But Rachel is a wonderful girl, and I'm confident that over time you'll come to love her too."

Morning light filtered through the living room curtains as Jim tried to focus on his breakfast. He felt an uneasy knot in his stomach. It was a familiar sensation, one that arose every time he shared the latest news from his life with his parents.

Today's news was genuinely positive; Jim had received a promotion at work. He shared the news enthusiastically with his mother and father, hoping to see a reflection of his joy in their eyes. However, their response was as predictable as ever.

"This still isn't the place where you could truly shine," his father said, looking perplexedly at his son.

His mother added, "I always said you should have pursued further studies."

Jim tried to brush off their comments, but they stung him deeply. He felt as if his accomplishments were diminished, that his parents would always find something to nitpick.

"Why does this happen? Why do even good news, when spoken by them, become a source of disappointment for me?" Jim pondered.

After breakfast, he decided to take a walk in the park. He felt he needed a break to clear his head. He realized that perhaps his parents just couldn't express their feelings and emotions properly, that their own fears and failures prevented them from seeing joy in their son's life.

Jim determined he'd need to find a way to communicate with his parents without letting their words affect his mood. But for now, he just wanted to savor the moment, relish the feeling of freedom, and the sense that he was moving in the right direction.

While strolling through the park, Jim called Rachel. His heart always raced a bit faster whenever he heard her voice. It was like a salve to the wounds after dealing with his parents.

"Hey, Rach," Jim said, his mood instantly lifted.

"Jim! How are you?" Her voice was warm and genuine.

"Well, you know, the usual parental remarks," he chuckled, "But let's not dwell on that. I have some news. I'm thinking of renting an apartment."

His words were like an invitation into his new life, a life where he could be himself without fear of criticism. Rachel was aware of this; he'd spoken about these plans before and had already saved up some money. Her response was full of understanding.

"That's wonderful, Jim! You deserve your own space, a place where you'll feel comfortable."

They chatted for a few more minutes, discussing various neighborhoods in the city and optimal choices for his budget. Rachel always supported him in every decision, and it empowered Jim to keep moving forward.

When the call ended, Jim sat on a bench, contemplating his future. He was filled with determination to take the next step. He had long dreamed of having his own place, and now, with Rachel's support and his own efforts, the moment had arrived.

The next day, Jim started browsing listings and calling real estate agents. He was excited and brimming with enthusiasm.

Jim's parents were emblematic of the "old school," brought up with distinct values and beliefs. To them, the ideal couple was constructed on shared interests, social status, and most significantly, a commonality in cultural and religious convictions. Rachel didn't fit this mold. Times change, and so do people's views. The younger generation has a different perspective, but many older individuals also show adaptability in these matters.

Rachel hailed from a different sociocultural background, holding unique life perspectives and an independent spirit. Her unpredictability and autonomy alarmed Jim's parents. They feared that Rachel might exert a detrimental influence on him or that their relationship could be volatile, potentially causing Jim pain.

Furthermore, Jim's parents struggled to grasp that the younger generation perceived relationships and love differently. For Jim, mutual understanding, sincerity, and support were paramount, far outweighing social or material considerations.

Additionally, parents sometimes fret over their children because of their personal fears and past experiences. Perhaps in the past, they encountered relationship disappointments or witnessed examples of failed unions among acquaintances. All these shaped their wary stance towards their son's new girlfriend.

While Jim's parents undoubtedly wished him happiness, their apprehensions and biases rendered their reactions to the news of his relationship with Rachel cautious and reserved.

They also typically exhibited several psychological processes and mechanisms:

1. Cognitive distortions. The parents had a biased view of the art world, believing that quality artistic education starts in childhood. This could have stemmed from widely accepted stereotypes or their personal experiences.

2. Defense Mechanisms. The remarks from Jim's mother and father might be manifestations of their own fears and apprehensions. Perhaps they worry that Jim might fail and end up disappointed. To shield him, they might try to "ground" his ambitions.

3. Projection. The parents might project onto Jim their own unrealized dreams or fears associated with failure. Possibly, they faced difficulties in the past when trying something new and now fear that their son might encounter the same challenges.

4. Emotional Estrangement. A lack of understanding or appreciation for their son's passions could be a result of emotional distance between Jim and his parents. There might have been past incidents leading to a loss of trust or closeness.

5. Limited Empathy. The parents might struggle to understand and accept Jim's feelings and emotions. This could be linked to their own emotional intelligence or circumstances that limit their empathetic capacities.

6. Envy. They might feel envious, fearing that Jim will manage to pursue his dreams, while they never learned how to chase theirs.

The parents' reaction to Jim's aspirations could stem from a myriad of factors, ranging from their own life experiences to defensive psychological mechanisms and cognitive biases.

Jim moved away from his parents, choosing to cut ties with those who seemed to drag him down. It's often futile to decipher why someone might hold negative sentiments towards you. If interacting with someone consistently dampens your mood or if they continually breach your personal boundaries, the cause might simply lie with them, not you. The most effective course of action could be to either cease communication altogether or limit it as much as possible.

Throughout our lives, we're constantly engaged in exchanges - we acquire knowledge, experience, and emotions, but we also leave an imprint. Yet, in these exchanges, we sometimes encounter individuals who contribute nothing positive to our lives, instead depleting our energy, self-belief, and joy. Such individuals can aptly be termed "toxic."

Toxic relationships can have a long-term negative impact on one's mental well-being. These relationships can drain your energy, undermine your self-esteem, and prevent you from realizing your full potential. It's vital for your psychological health and overall happiness to recognize when you're in such a relationship and take steps to distance yourself or set boundaries.

Toxic people are those who consistently express resentment, criticism, doubt your abilities, belittle you, and evoke constant feelings of guilt in you. Their negative influence can stealthily seep into your soul, eroding your self-confidence and planting seeds of doubt and fear. They have a knack for pressing down, criticizing, and shattering your dreams and aspirations. And, unfortunately, these individuals often disguise themselves as close friends or family members who "just care about you."

Why is it so hard for us to break away from toxic individuals? Several reasons might hold us back:

1. Fear of Loneliness. For many, the fear of being alone feels worse than enduring toxic relationships.

2. Low Self-esteem. If one's self-worth is low, they might feel as though they deserve this treatment or believe no one else would want to be with them.

3. Habit. In some cases, interacting with toxic people becomes routine. We might get so accustomed to a particular lifestyle that we fail to realize there are other healthier options.

4. Family Ties. Toxic individuals can sometimes be family members, and distancing oneself might feel like betrayal or a disregard for familial values.

5. Social Pressure. Society often pressures us to maintain relationships, even if they're harmful.

6. Financial Dependence. In some instances, people remain in toxic relationships due to financial or material dependency.

7. Hope for Change. Many hold the belief that they can change a toxic individual or that the person will eventually transform over time.

8. Lack of Awareness. Some might not recognize the toxicity of their relationships simply because they lack the experience of healthier relationships for comparison.

To foster a psychologically healthy environment, it's crucial to recognize and understand why we might stay in toxic relationships. This self-awareness is the first step to seeking ways to overcome and move beyond them. Taking control and prioritizing your well-being over maintaining a detrimental relationship is essential for personal growth and achieving mental peace.

Interacting with toxic individuals can wreak havoc on one's personal life, mental, and even physical health. Here are some potential consequences:

1. Emotional Drain. Constant interaction with a toxic person can lead to feelings of fatigue, apathy, and irritability.

2. Decreased Self-worth. Toxic individuals often criticize and belittle others, which can lower one's self-esteem.

3. Stress. Constant conflicts, arguments, and dramas can elevate stress levels.

4. Reduced Productivity. If a toxic person is in your professional circle, it can impact your work efficiency and motivation.

5. Physical Ailments. Chronic stress, resulting from interaction with toxic people, can lead to physical issues such as insomnia, digestive problems, high blood pressure, and weakened immunity.

6. Isolation. In avoiding toxic individuals, you might become less socially active, losing social connections and relationships.

7. Relationship Strains. Toxic individuals can incite conflicts between you and others, sometimes creating rifts in friendships and romantic relationships.

8. Eroded Self-Identity. Constant criticism and manipulation from a toxic person can make you question your values, beliefs, and interests.

9. Increased Anxiety. The constant anticipation of the next conflict or criticism can induce a state of persistent anxiety.

10. Worsened Mental Health. In the long run, interactions with toxic individuals can contribute to the development of depression, anxiety disorders, or other mental health issues.

Sometimes, we might not even recognize the harm these interactions bring into our lives. However, it's essential to understand that the absence of a toxic individual in your life is far more beneficial than their presence. Recognizing the adverse effects and actively working to either set boundaries or eliminate such relationships is crucial for one's overall well-being.

Who Should You Consider Distancing Yourself From?

1. People who don't celebrate your successes. If someone regularly shows jealousy or tries to diminish your achievements, they might not be a true friend.

2. Those who use you for their own gain. If someone communicates with you only when they need something, it's a clear sign of toxicity.

3. People who leave you feeling guilty after interactions. A genuine friend would never make you feel bad about their issues or mistakes.

4. Those who disrespect your boundaries. If someone disregards your "no" or ignores your feelings and needs, that's also toxic behavior.

Recognizing a toxic individual can be challenging since every person has unique traits and behavioral patterns. However, there are several common indicators of toxicity:

1. Criticism and belittlement. Toxic individuals often criticize others, aiming to belittle their achievements, opinions, or appearance.

2. Manipulation. Such people might use various tactics to get you to do what they want, including guilt, threats, or emotional manipulation.

3. Inconsistency. They might be very sweet and amiable one moment, and aggressive and hostile the next.

4. Disrespect of boundaries. Toxic individuals often overlook or violate others' personal boundaries, be it physical, emotional, or psychological.

5. Victim mentality. They often portray themselves as victims, shifting the blame of their issues onto others.

6. Lack of accountability. Toxic individuals seldom acknowledge their mistakes or accept responsibility for their actions.

7. Envy. They might be envious of others' successes or achievements and attempt to downplay their importance.

8. Excessive drama. Their lives are frequently filled with conflicts and disputes, and they often involve other people in them.

9. Avoidance of truth. They might frequently lie or distort facts to appear better or avoid responsibility.

10. Emotional drain. Interacting with them leaves you feeling drained, tired, or stressed. Always and everywhere, your feelings serve as crucial indicators—trust them.

It's essential to understand that every individual is unique. Not everyone who exhibits one or two of these signs is necessarily toxic. However, if you notice several of these behavioral traits in someone around you, it's wise to tread carefully and consider setting boundaries in your relationship with them.

How should you approach such individuals? The first realization is that every person has the right to their boundaries. If you feel someone is infringing on yours, it's crucial to take action. Set those boundaries. Don't be afraid to say "no" and stand up for your interests. If someone continues to cross your limits, perhaps it's time to re-evaluate your relationship with them.

It's vital to remember that distancing oneself from toxic relationships isn't a sign of weakness; rather, it's an act of self-care and preserving your mental peace. You deserve happiness and to be surrounded by supportive people.

Throughout our lives, we inevitably encounter various individuals. Some leave behind bright, warm memories, while others cast shadows of unpleasant moments.

However, not all recognize that as we journey through life, we also leave our mark. It's essential that this mark be a positive one.

A person who is toxic for you might not be the same for another; perhaps the particular dynamics between you both lead to such outcomes.

Often, we don't consider that we might be the source of negativity for others. We're so focused on protecting ourselves that we overlook how our actions or words could hurt others. A moment of reflection on this can highlight the importance of not just taking but also giving in relationships.

So, when you sense toxicity from someone, remember: your response is your choice. You can choose to distance yourself, set boundaries, or even end the relationship if it's for your well-being. However, it's also crucial to recognize your role in these dynamics. Aim to spread kindness, understanding, and warmth wherever you go. This approach will not only enrich your life but will also make the world a slightly better place.

CHAPTER SEVEN

Never Settle for What You've Achieved. What Might Hold You Back on the Path to Success?

Jim strolled through the city at his usual pace. His ears were immersed in the tunes of his favorite songs when a vivid poster outside a café grabbed his attention. "Mural Design and Creation Contest: Transform Urban Spaces!" the headline read. The idea enchanted Jim. He had long been fascinated by street art and even tried his hand at creating small pieces on abandoned buildings around the area. This contest offered an opportunity to showcase his talent on large, visible city walls.

Without hesitation, Jim pulled out his smartphone and began filling in the online application form. His mind buzzed with ideas about the design he wanted to create, the story he wished to share with the city. After all, murals are more than just paint on walls; they're stories, emotions, and moments captured in time.

He could already envision his artwork coming to life on one of the city's central walls. His idea was vibrant, dynamic, and most importantly, unique. "The whole city will see my contest piece," he thought, the realization making his heart skip a beat.

As he penned down the final lines of his application, a wave of pride and excitement washed over him. He immediately texted Rachel, "Guess what I just did?"

A few moments later, Rachel replied, "What, dear?"

"I applied for a mural design contest for city walls. And I got in!" Jim texted back with enthusiasm.

"Wow, that's amazing! What are you planning to depict?" Rachel inquired.

The Secrets of Living

Jim paused before replying. Her question stirred something deep within him, prompting him to reflect on his inner world and the story he wished to convey through his art. "You know, Rach, it's more than just a painting on a wall. It's a chance to share something meaningful, to convey emotions and make people think. I need time to come up with an idea that's both creative and profound," he wrote.

Rachel responded with understanding, "I believe in you, Jim. You'll find your muse. Meanwhile, we can brainstorm some ideas together tonight."

Jim smiled as he read the message. He felt grateful for Rachel's support. Yet, he also recognized that the responsibility for the mural's theme and quality was squarely on his shoulders.

That evening, at Jim's apartment, he and Rachel began brainstorming. Before them lay a notepad and an array of colored pens. Rachel sketched out several concepts: cityscapes, portraits, abstract designs.

"How about a concept of 'merging city and nature'?" Rachel suggested, sketching a tree whose roots morphed into city buildings.

"It's intriguing," Jim replied, slightly frowning, "but it seems a tad cliché."

Rachel shrugged and continued her sketching. "What about representing people of diverse backgrounds, holding hands in a circle?"

Jim pondered for a moment. "It's a nice idea, but I'm looking for something more unique. Something that truly captures the essence and spirit of our city."

Rachel smiled, "You've always set such high standards for yourself."

They both laughed but soon returned to their thoughts. The soft hum of a lamp filled the room, creating a cozy atmosphere.

"You know, Rach," Jim began, staring at the blank sheet before him, "sometimes I feel the answer is right in front of us, just hidden. We just need the right perspective to see it."

For Jim, it was crucial to create something meaningful. This mural wasn't just a wall; it was his calling card, his chance to express himself and convey his feelings, dreams, and ideas to the townsfolk. It was also a potential financial boon.

"What about a historical depiction of our city? From ancient times to present?" Rachel proposed, sketching a quick draft.

"It's good," Jim countered, "but it might be too cluttered. And townspeople see that every day."

Recognizing his determination for something unparalleled, Rachel suggested, "Perhaps we should move away from specific images and focus on emotions? Like a rainbow made of human silhouettes, showcasing the diversity and unity of our town's residents?"

Jim paused, deep in thought. "I like your sentiment about emotions, but the rainbow idea... it might be too simplistic."

Both continued to pitch ideas, each met with critique from the other. Jim started to feel the weight of the situation. The entire town would see his work, and he wanted it to be perfect.

"I think we should take a break and revisit this tomorrow," he suggested.

"You're right," Rachel agreed, massaging her temples. "We need some rest, and maybe inspiration will strike on its own."

They settled on the couch, wrapped in each other's arms, and flipped on the TV, trying to distract from the issue that weighed heavily on Jim. But he knew that he would have to face it again tomorrow.

The Secrets of Living

Morning sunlight danced on the breakfast that Rachel had just prepared. The aroma of coffee and waffles added to the cozy ambiance. However, a look of concern was evident on Jim's face.

"Any ideas for the mural yet?" Rachel inquired, her gaze dropping to her plate.

Jim nodded pensively. "I tossed and turned all night trying to think of something unique and standout. But I drew a blank. Maybe this isn't for me?"

Rachel took his hand. "Jim, you can't just give up. We both know how talented you are. There are times when inspiration is elusive, but it's temporary."

He looked at her and managed a faint smile. "I still have the option to back out of the contest. I don't want to rush something or be disingenuous. People will see this mural daily. It needs to be special."

"That's precisely why you shouldn't back out," Rachel responded. "There's still time. I believe you'll soon have your idea."

Jim seemed contemplative. "I'm not so sure..."

"Please tell me, what's really bothering you?"

Jim sighed, locking eyes with her. "I'm scared, Rach. The whole town will see my work. What if they don't like it? What if I can't convey my idea? Maybe I was mistaken to think this was my calling."

Rachel looked at him with understanding. "Your anxiety is natural. It's because you care about your work. But you're too hard on yourself."

Jim frowned, "I just don't want to let anyone down. Maybe I should let go of this mural idea. It will consume a lot of time. Time I could spend taking extra shifts with the painting crew where I know what I'm doing."

Rachel leaned in, "Jim, you have a unique gift. And you shouldn't hide it because you're afraid of not meeting expectations. Every artist goes through this. Look, I'm not the one entering the contest and my perspective might be biased since I'm your girlfriend. But I think you shouldn't worry too much; it's about taking part and gaining the experience. Let's pick a feasible idea, preferably one that isn't too complex to implement."

"But I want it to be perfect," Jim replied.

"Perfection is a process," Rachel countered. "You can't create something perfect on your first try. But you can create something unique and genuine. That's the essence of art."

After a thoughtful pause, Jim said, "You know what, you're right. Maybe I've been too fixated on this. I've made mistakes in life, one more or less doesn't make much difference. And I think I'd regret not trying more than if the mural isn't well received. I'll take a day off and wander the city streets looking for inspiration."

Rachel smiled, "Now that sounds like a plan! In the meantime, let's enjoy our morning."

Jim nodded, sipping his coffee, "Thanks for being here. Without you, I might've given up by now."

Rachel softly smiled back, "That's what I'm here for."

Prisoners of Our Own Convictions: How Our Limitations Stifle Growth.

Personal barriers - these invisible chains that restrict our potential - are often self imposed by our very imagination. The human psyche has a remarkable ability to create barriers, ones that can sometimes be far more formidable than tangible ones. Many fear making mistakes, being the subject of ridicule or criticism, and thus choose to stay within their comfort zones. But what if we dared to venture beyond?

Psychology suggests that our limitations are often shaped by past experiences. For instance, if a child was scolded for a mistake, they might grow up to be a perfectionist, fearing even the smallest misstep.

However insurmountable these internal barriers may seem, they can be broken. The first step is acknowledgment. As soon as we recognize and desire to overcome these hindrances, our brain begins to look for solutions. Next, is taking proactive measures. One can start small. The hardest part isn't overcoming the barrier but taking that initial leap of faith. Once you realize that your internal "I can't" is merely an illusion, a world of limitless opportunities unfolds before you.

It's vital to remember: We are the masters of our thoughts, and only we can determine whether they'll aid us or become obstacles in our path to success.

People often say that the past can't be changed. But what if, in reality, it can? Not literally, of course, but in how we perceive and interpret our past events.

Self-reflection is a crucial tool for anyone wishing to transform their life. It's a process of internal dialogue where one questions their actions, motives, and feelings.

Each of our pasts isn't just a sequence of events; it's a narrative that we repeatedly tell ourselves. And this story influences our present state, our self-perception, our relations with others, and our worldview.

Begin by analyzing your past. Ask yourself a simple question: "What story lies behind my actions and decisions?" Perhaps, behind your fears, there is a childhood trauma or an old belief that you are not worthy of better. Understanding the roots of these beliefs is the first step to overcoming them.

Through self-reflection, you can "rewrite" your story. Not by changing events, but by altering your perception and interpretation of them. An event that once seemed like a tragedy can become a valuable experience, a lesson, or even a turning point in your life.

However, don't think that this process is simple and quick. On the contrary, it takes time, effort, and sometimes the support of a professional. But the results are worth it. When you stop being a prisoner of your past, new horizons and opportunities will open up before you.

Your past is a part of you, but it doesn't define your future. Self-reflection and awareness of your past provide the key to creating a new story in which you are the main character, in control of your destiny.

Changing yourself is a journey, and every traveler needs the right tools. On the path to understanding and transforming your "self," you may need a whole arsenal of methods.

1. Self-Reflection Journal.

Start by creating a simple journal where you can record your thoughts, feelings, and attempt to analyze your behavior. This tool will help you see patterns, understand the reasons behind certain actions, and learn to control them.

2. Meditation and Mindfulness.

Meditation is not just a trendy practice; it's a method of working with your consciousness. It teaches you to be "here and now," to listen to yourself and your inner world. This tool will help you improve concentration, reduce stress, and gain a better understanding of yourself.

3. Affirmations.

These are short statements that help reprogram your brain in a positive way. For example, "I am worthy of success and happiness." The key is to repeat them regularly and genuinely believe in the words you speak.

4. Visualization.

Try to visualize your life as you would like it to be. This method helps you "paint" a picture of your future, set goals, and understand what you truly want.

5. Working with a Psychologist.

A professional can help you see what you might be missing. They will provide you with the necessary tools and methods, as well as assist you in finding solutions to complex issues.

Reading books, attending lectures, and participating in workshops are all part of expanding your horizons and discovering new possibilities when you immerse yourself in the world of knowledge.

Every individual is unique, and what works for one may not work for another. However, it's essential to remember that the path to change begins with the first step. Don't be afraid to seek your own methods, experiment, and find what genuinely works for you.

Common Personal Limitations That Often Hinder Success.

1. Low Self-Esteem. Self-doubt can block the path to achieving your goals. Self-esteem is the opinion a person holds about themselves. Low self-esteem can become a barrier to self-realization, the attainment of desired goals, and life happiness.

Low self-esteem often has its roots in childhood. Criticism from parents, teachers, or peers can leave a lasting impact. Negative life events, such as failures, parental divorce, or the loss of a loved one, can also contribute to reduced self-esteem. Individuals with low self-esteem often avoid new tasks and challenges, fearing mistakes. They may excessively worry about others' opinions and judgments.

The first step in overcoming low self-esteem is awareness. It's crucial to understand that your worth as a person is not determined by past mistakes or others' opinions. Surround yourself with people who believe in you and provide support. Avoid relationships that amplify your doubts and indecision.

2. Fear of Failure.

The fear of failure can often prevent us from trying something new or taking risks. This fear is frequently rooted in early childhood experiences. It can result from constant criticism, the high expectations of others, or past failures and disappointments. As a result, individuals may start believing that they are unworthy of success and that it's better not to try at all than to face the possibility of failure. People who experience a fear of failure often avoid new challenges, risky situations, or they may procrastinate or even refuse to start something out of fear of making mistakes. This leads to a reduction in life experiences, missed opportunities, and unrealized potential achievements.

It's crucial to understand that every failure is an opportunity for growth. Mistakes and setbacks are essential for personal development. Rather than viewing them as catastrophes, they should be seen as valuable lessons.

3. Procrastination.

Procrastination, the act of delaying or postponing tasks despite understanding the possible negative consequences of such delays, can lead to missed opportunities.

Procrastination is one of the most common issues faced by modern individuals. We're all familiar with the feeling when essential tasks are continuously put off, and the moment of "later" never seems to arrive. Often, the fear of failure, perfectionism, or a lack of motivation underlies procrastination. Unclear goals can also make a task seem unattractive or difficult. By procrastinating, we miss out on many opportunities, face the need to work at an accelerated pace, experience stress, and feelings of guilt.

Strategies to overcome procrastination:

- Task Breakdown: Breaking down a large task into smaller steps makes it less intimidating.

- Pomodoro Technique: Work for 25 minutes and then take a 5-minute break. This helps you stay focused and prevents burnout.

- Visualization of Results: Imagine how you will feel when the task is completed.

- Celebrate Achievements: Acknowledge completed tasks. This boosts confidence and motivation to keep going.

Understanding what truly matters to you helps you concentrate your efforts and reduces distractions. Procrastination is not a life sentence; it simply indicates that there is room for growth and improvement in your time and task management skills. As you develop, you become more focused, productive, and satisfied with your work results.

4. Inability to Set and Follow Goals. One of the main obstacles to personal and professional growth is the lack of well-defined goals. Without them, it's like sailing a ship without a compass; it's challenging to determine your direction and the purpose of your actions. A goal is not just a desired outcome; it's a map that shows the path to what you want. Before setting goals, ask yourself, "What do I truly want?" Understanding your genuine needs and desires will help you set the right priorities.

Clearly define what you want to achieve. Establish criteria by which you can evaluate your progress. Choose a goal that you can realistically attain with the resources and opportunities you have. Ensure that the goal aligns with your long term plans and desires. Set deadlines for achieving your goals.

Big tasks can be intimidating due to their scale. Divide your goal into small achievable steps. This not only simplifies the process but also provides a sense of accomplishment at each stage. Regularly assess your progress, adjust your plan as needed, and celebrate your achievements.

The ability to set and follow goals is a key skill that can guarantee your success. By learning and improving this skill, you become more focused, productive, and confident in your abilities.

5. Resistance to New Ideas. Rejecting new ideas or technologies can limit growth and development.

6. Poor Time Management. This can lead to a loss of focus on priority tasks.

7. Fear of Criticism. The fear of being judged can hinder stepping outside your comfort zone. People interact extensively with the social world around them, and this world often becomes a source of fears and anxieties. The fear of criticism is one of the most common, and it can significantly restrict an individual's potential.

The fear of criticism often takes root in childhood or adolescence when feedback and evaluations from adults or peers may have led to feelings of vulnerability or shame. It's important to differentiate between constructive criticism, which aims to help and develop, and condemnation, which can be negative and destructive. The more self-assured you become, the less fear or apprehension criticism provokes. Work on your self-improvement and recognize your uniqueness and significance as an antidote to the fear of criticism. Consider criticism as an opportunity for growth and development. Accept it as information that can help you become better.

Surround yourself with people who support you and believe in your abilities. Avoid toxic relationships where criticism is used as a means of manipulation or destruction. Learn to analyze critical remarks without emotions. Evaluate them objectively: is there any rational basis for them, should you pay attention to them, or can you ignore them? Realize that nobody is perfect. Every person has their weaknesses, and that's okay. The fear of criticism is a natural feeling that everyone experiences. But armed with the right tools and understanding, you can transform this fear into a powerful motivator for growth and self-improvement.

8. Perfectionism. Distorted pursuit of perfection can be both a motivator for growth and a stumbling block on the path to self-realization. Striving for high-quality work and taking tasks seriously are generally positive qualities. However, if this pursuit of perfection is driven by a fear of criticism, making mistakes, and the subsequent judgment of others, leading to stress and frustration, then such destructive perfectionism becomes a problem. It hinders productivity and can negatively impact one's psychological well-being.

Perfectionism often originates in childhood when children are constantly told they must be better and achieve more. Under such pressure, the drive for perfection can become obsessive. Behind these excessive demands on oneself often lies the fear of not being worthy or of not meeting others' or one's expectations. It's essential to learn to distinguish between real standards and unrealistic expectations. Perfection is an illusion, and it's crucial to learn to recognize this illusion. Mistakes are a part of the learning and development process. Instead of fearing them, view mistakes as opportunities for growth. You need to know when to say "enough," realizing that you've done your best, and that's good enough.

Learn to let go of the idea of perfection and accept yourself as you are, valuing your achievements and your ability to learn from your mistakes.

9. Comparing Yourself to Others. This can lead to feelings of inadequacy or envy. When we compare ourselves to others, we often make the mistake of thinking that others are more successful, smarter, or happier than us. Such thoughts can undermine our self-esteem and motivation. We only see the external side of other people's lives, their successes and joys, while their difficulties and failures remain hidden. This misconception can lead to a distorted perception of reality. Each person has their own life path, starting conditions, and opportunities. By comparing ourselves to others, we forget that each of us is unique. When we compare ourselves, we often focus on what we lack rather than what we have. This can lead to feelings of inadequacy and missed opportunities. Envy can be useful if it becomes a source of inspiration for personal development and goal achievement.

Try shifting your focus from comparing yourself to others to comparing yourself to your past self. Instead of looking at others, evaluate your progress and achievements. If you do compare yourself to someone, let it be a source of inspiration rather than disappointment. Think about what positive traits or qualities you'd like to develop in yourself when looking at that person. Comparing yourself to others is a natural process, but it's essential to do it consciously and constructively. Recognize and appreciate your uniqueness. Nobody in the world can be a better version of you than yourself.

10. Information Overload. In the era of the internet, it's easy to get lost among the multitude of advice and recommendations.

11. Avoiding Responsibility for Your Mistakes. This can lead to repeating the same mistakes. Taking responsibility for your actions is a key aspect of personal

growth. When we avoid admitting our mistakes, we deprive ourselves of valuable experience and the opportunity to learn from the past. Often, our minds create defense mechanisms to protect us from pain or shame. As a result, we deny our mistakes or look for scapegoats among those around us. Acknowledging your mistakes makes you vulnerable to others, and this fear can be a barrier to self-awareness. Every mistake is an opportunity for learning. By taking responsibility, we begin to understand what we could have done differently and learn to avoid similar mistakes in the future. We also learn to forgive ourselves and others, developing a sense of compassion and understanding.

When we recognize and accept our weaknesses, it enhances our capacity for self-reflection and allows us to better understand ourselves. By being sincere and honest with ourselves and others, we create a foundation for trusting relationships in both our personal and professional lives.

12. Approval-Seeking. Constantly striving to please others can hinder you from following your own path. Each of us wants to feel loved, valued, and recognized. However, when the pursuit of approval begins to dominate our lives, we risk losing our individuality and inner balance. If a child did not receive enough attention or approval from their parents, they may grow up seeking these feelings from others. The desire to please everyone can lead to the loss of one's own interests, desires, and goals. Life begins to be built on other people's expectations rather than one's own aspirations.

The first step in overcoming this dependency is awareness. Ask yourself: "Am I doing this for myself or to seek approval?" Gradually, teach yourself to act in accordance with your own desires and beliefs, and learn to be confident in your decisions. Acknowledge your achievements and allow yourself to take pride in them.

13. Victim Mentality. When a person constantly sees themselves as a victim, they often experience feelings of helplessness, believing that circumstances or other people control their lives. This thinking style can arise from past traumas or beliefs instilled in childhood. Living in the role of a "victim," a person loses the opportunity to take responsibility for their life. This can lead to stagnation, loss of motivation, and a lack of personal growth. It's essential to stop focusing on how the world "wronged" you and start looking for ways to influence your destiny. Analyze your thoughts and beliefs. Ask yourself: "Why do I feel this way? Are there real reasons to think that I cannot change my life?" Even if tragic events have occurred in your life, you still have the choice of how to respond to them. By taking responsibility for your decisions and actions, you gain control over your future. If your victim mentality is related to past traumas, consider seeking help from a professional. Professional assistance can provide you with tools to work through these feelings. Avoid people or situations that reinforce your "victim" role. Seeking support from those who believe in your ability to overcome obstacles will be more productive.

14. Inability to Say "No". We've all experienced moments when we're afraid or unwilling to say no to people, even if it comes at the expense of our time, resources, or well-being. Often, the roots of this behavior trace back to childhood when a child might have been indoctrinated with the belief that they should always be helpful, kind, and accommodating to others. The inability to say "no" can lead to overload, stress, wasting time on unimportant matters, and missing out on significant opportunities.

Ask yourself questions: "Why did I agree to this? What am I afraid of? What will happen if I decline?" Identify what truly matters to you and learn to set boundaries. Start small by refusing small requests that don't align with your preferences. The more you practice, the easier it becomes to say "no" in more complex situations.

Refusal doesn't have to be abrupt or rude. You can learn to decline tactfully by explaining your decisions. Be prepared for not everyone to understand or accept your decision to decline something. That's okay. Some may even try to make you feel guilty for saying no. Your well-being and your time are a priority.

15. Limiting Beliefs. Stereotypes and internal convictions that don't align with reality. These are mental barriers or convictions that a person recognizes as truth about themselves, other people, or the world around them, even if they are not based on reality. Here are some examples of such beliefs:

   - Doubt in One's Abilities: "I'm not smart enough to study at a prestigious university."

   - Fear of the New: "It's too late for me to change anything in my life."

   - Undervaluing One's Experience: "I have no experience, so I can't apply for this job."

   - Gender Stereotypes: "Men don't cry" or "Women shouldn't engage in strenuous physical work."

   - Fear of Criticism: "I better not share my opinion to avoid being judged."

   - Attachment to the Past: "I've always been a failure, and nothing will change."

   - Self-Harm: "I deserve this pain/problem because I'm a bad person."

   - Financial Stereotypes: "Money corrupts people" or "I will never have a lot of money."

16. Lack of Emotional Resilience. Emotions are a powerful tool that can either help you achieve your goals or lead to failure. Have you ever experienced a situation where sadness or anger overwhelmed you, making it difficult to focus on your tasks?

Or perhaps you've made a decision solely based on emotions without considering facts and logic?

Emotional resilience is the ability to remain calm and focused in challenging situations, not allowing emotions to dictate your decisions. It doesn't mean suppressing emotions but rather managing them. For example, you may feel upset about a work failure, but instead of withdrawing or falling into despair, you use that emotion as motivation for further efforts and finding new solutions. However, not everyone possesses this kind of resilience. For many, every emotional outburst becomes a cause for concern and procrastination of important decisions.

Overcoming these limitations requires self-awareness, reflection, and often the help of professionals or therapists. But recognizing your limitations is the first step towards overcoming them. It's the necessary action without which positive change is impossible, except in critical situations when a person must act without much thought.

CHAPTER EIGHT

Unwritten Traditions

Golden sunlight kissed the old brick wall at the street corner, where Jim labored over his mural. It was his masterpiece, his narrative, his lens into the world. The draft he'd meticulously prepared showcased a cityscape where the old and new intertwined, crafting a distinct character.

Rachel had been his rock throughout this venture. Not only did she assist with color selections, but she also played the roles of his critic, confidant, and at times, muse. Her refined taste and keen sense of style worked wonders.

"Do you think this is too bright?" Jim asked, pointing to the vivid blue he was using to depict the old railway station.

Rachel squinted, appraising the composition. "Maybe a shade darker to blend in with the overall backdrop? But I love the vibe. It adds a spark to the whole painting."

Jim nodded, mixing the paint, aiming for the right hue. The mural became more than just a task for him, it was an avenue for self-expression. Every brushstroke on the wall made his soul swell with joy and serenity.

Every so often, passersby would halt and admire the evolving artwork. Some inquired, some simply smiled, while others shared personal stories of their lives intertwining with the depicted landmarks or landscapes. With each day, the mural grew more vibrant and telling.

Apart from his contest work, Jim continued his regular painting job. The construction site was a constant hum of activity. Engrossed in his work, Jim was jolted by a disgruntled voice near the entrance of the construction trailer. Drawing closer, he recognized the voice of his foreman, Robert, and an irate client, William, who was rumored to be notoriously picky.

"I gave explicit instructions!" William bellowed, his face turning beet-red. "Is this your idea of quality work?"

Robert, standing by the construction plan, replied calmly, "Mr. William, I understand your concerns. Let's pinpoint where you believe we've gone astray."

With a smirk, William retorted, "Gone astray? GONE ASTRAY? Are you mocking me? Perhaps someone more competent than you is in order?"

Maintaining his composure, Robert continued, "I respect your viewpoint and am ready to address specific issues. Our goal is to get everything right."

William smirked sardonically, "Or maybe, just maybe, you're not up to the task? Should I be looking for another company?"

"We value you as a client," Robert responded with genuine respect, "and are prepared to meet halfway to satisfy your demands. What exactly concerns you?"

A flicker of surprise flashed in William's eyes; he probably hadn't expected such a response. Trying to regain the upper hand, he countered, "You just seem afraid to admit your mistakes!"

"If they exist, we'll address and rectify them," Robert stated firmly.

For a moment, William hesitated, then, with evident reluctance, handed over a list of grievances.

From the sidelines, Jim observed the exchange, awed by Robert's patience and professionalism. When William departed, he approached his foreman, "You really know how to handle people, even aggressive ones."

"Jim," Robert began, "the key is standing up for yourself without infringing on the rights of others. Never stoop to the aggressor's level, and you'll maintain control over the situation. It's a skill that comes with experience."

After William's exit, Jim's gaze lingered on Robert, drawing parallels with his father and how he used to handle disputes. Jim had faced confrontations both at work and in life, often finding himself torn between the urge to retaliate and the apprehension of consequences.

He remembered a school incident where a classmate, Max, constantly teased him. Jim felt compelled to stand up, defend his honor. But each time he tried to voice his feelings, words got caught in his throat, and he'd retreat silently, masking his emotions. He often pondered why he reacted that way. His father's approach to conflicts always oscillated between aggression or silence. Jim had never seen a middle ground between these extremes and remained uncertain about finding it.

Reflecting on his childhood, vivid memories of his father confronting adversaries or injustice sprang to Jim's mind. His father, a muscular and volatile man, frequently resorted to aggressive outbursts. Whenever he faced criticism or disputes, he'd instantly go on the defensive, often leading to heated arguments and scenes. Yet, at times, especially if the adversary seemed more powerful, his father would retract, becoming introspective, leaving the family in a cloud of unease and tension.

In stark contrast stood Robert, embodying an entirely different approach. He was firm yet composed, always open to dialogue even in the face of acute stress. Observing Robert, Jim discerned an alternative way of addressing conflicts, one that preserved self-respect and trust.

How different would his life have been if his father possessed communication skills akin to Robert's? Would his childhood have been less fraught? Perhaps, his relationship with his father could have been deeper, more connected?

"Jim," Robert broke into his thoughts, "I'd wager that in the end, William will drop at least half of those complaints. He's one of those who just loves to stir the pot. The key is not to fall for his provocations and stay the course calmly."

Jim nodded in agreement, truly taken aback by Robert's keen insight and unwavering stance.

Jim and Rachel walked through the aisles of a home improvement store, selecting materials for their mural project. They laughed and joked, discussing various paint shades, when suddenly their mirth was interrupted by a loud, mocking voice.

"Oh, look who's here! Jimmy, good old Jimmy!" Larry called out, standing amid the paint section, his eyes fixed maliciously on Rachel. His gaze was challenging and unkind.

Rachel took a step back, giving Larry a displeased look. She felt uneasy under his scrutiny.

"Jim, is this guy a friend of yours?" she asked, trying to sound calm.

"That's Larry. We went to school together," Jim replied, trying to maintain his composure. He remembered all the taunts and nitpicks from Larry.

"So, Jim, still drawing those silly pictures? And your girlfriend's helping you now?" Larry sneered, moving closer to Rachel.

Jim took a deep breath, trying to remain calm. "Larry, we're just here to buy supplies for our project. We didn't come here to chat with you," he responded peacefully.

Larry laughed. "You're still the same, Jim. Always trying to avoid trouble. But you think I'll just let your girlfriend off that easy?"

Jim took another deep breath. "Larry, I'm asking you to be respectful. We're not here to argue with you."

"And what if I don't want to be?" Larry retorted mockingly.

"If you try anything that might harm us, I'll call the police right away. And don't you dare speak to me in that tone," Jim said firmly, taking Rachel by the hand.

Larry hesitated for a moment, his smirk fading slightly. "Fine, Jim. But remember, it's a small world. We'll meet again."

Jim and Rachel quickly made their purchases and left the store, doing their best to ignore Larry.

"You were so confident, Jim. I'm proud of you," Rachel smiled.

"Thanks, Rach. I just didn't want to play into his games. It's not worth it," Jim replied.

If the traditions you were raised in compel you to harm yourself, for instance, to get into a fight in response to an insult, it's time to question those traditions.

Traditions shape our culture, our worldview, and our sense of self. They serve us, helping to mark significant life moments and strengthening familial and societal bonds. However, some of these traditions may be outdated or even harmful. When traditions become a burden or threaten your well-being, it might be wise to reconsider them.

Commitments to culture or traditions should not put you in a position where you have to choose between your safety and dignity. Your health, safety, and psychological well-being should always come first.

If you encounter a tradition that limits you or causes harm, consider asking yourself the following questions:

1. Why does this tradition exist? How does it serve me?

2. What would happen if I chose not to follow this tradition?

3. Are there other ways I can honor my culture or values without putting myself at risk?

No tradition, no matter how ancient or revered, should endanger or harm you. Don't be afraid to be true to yourself and to do what's right for you. Traditions evolve, and if they don't serve you, perhaps it's time to change them or craft your own.

In every society, there are unspoken destructive traditions or behavioral norms that can negatively impact an individual or the community at large. Some of these traditions include:

1. Taboos against speaking out. In some cultures, individuals are taught not to openly voice their opinions, especially if they diverge from popular views. This can suppress creativity and innovation.

2. "Toxic masculinity". A destructive belief where men are expected to always be strong, emotionless, and take charge.

3. Traditional gender roles. Expecting women to handle household chores and men to work can limit the potential and opportunities of both.

4. Bullying and Mockery. While some communities may view bullying as a "rite of passage," the truth is that it can leave profound emotional scars.

5. Forced Marriages. In certain cultures, it's customary for girls to be married off without their consent.

6. Pursuit of the "Ideal" Body. Societal pressures to conform to specific beauty standards can lead to mental and physical health issues and can diminish self-worth.

7. Envy and Rivalry. There's a prevailing belief in some societies that one person's success comes at the expense of another. As a result, successful individuals might be viewed negatively, deterring others from pursuing their own goals.

8. Concealing Psychological Issues. In many cultures, admitting to mental health problems is stigmatized as a sign of weakness, preventing individuals from seeking professional help.

9. Silent Consent. The widely held belief of "mind your own business" can lead to the overlooking or even endorsement of various forms of violence or harassment.

10. Fear of "Losing Face". In certain cultures, the fear of losing social status or reputation can lead to the concealment of mistakes or oversights. It can also compel individuals to respond in specific ways to imposed conflicts, becoming a tool for the dominant to dictate terms to the less powerful.

11. Age Stereotypes. Expecting people of a certain age to behave in a predefined manner can limit their life opportunities or ambitions.

12. Accepting Alcoholism as the Norm. In some societies, regular and excessive alcohol consumption is seen as typical or even a mark of true masculinity or femininity.

13. Sexuality Taboos. An avoidance of discussing sexuality can hamper sexual health education and the prevention of sexually transmitted infections.

14. Family Secrets. Some families harbor secrets or issues that are deemed "unspeakable" even within the family unit, leading to oppression and trauma.

15. Contempt for the "Others". Showing disdain for those different in culture, religion, gender, or sexual orientation can foster discrimination and violence.

Keep in mind, many worthy individuals left this world prematurely due to adhering to these unwritten "traditions". Some entered conflicts and lost their lives, others crashed their cars attempting to not be overtaken by road bullies, some excessively consumed alcohol because it was tradition, and they felt they couldn't refuse friends or family. Others, due to tradition, refrained from seeking medical care. I urge you to take a clear look at the traditions that form your daily life and, if any of them bring harm or have the potential to, refrain from adhering to them.

When it comes to unwritten traditions, it's essential to realize that society and its members might not be receptive to someone's refusal to follow them. Merely recognizing their destructiveness isn't enough. Rejecting a "tradition" will likely provoke a confrontational situation. So, how do you navigate such circumstances effectively and without adverse outcomes? The answer lies in the skills of assertive communication.

Assertive Communication.

In conflict situations, assertive communication is a set of skills that assist an individual in defending their interests, expressing their feelings and opinions without violating others' rights. In turn, this approach doesn't give additional reasons to escalate the conflict.

I-statements. Expressing your feelings and reactions without blaming the other side. Instead of saying, "You're annoying me!", it's more constructive to state, "I feel upset when you constantly interrupt me." This way, you're verbalizing your feelings without putting the blame on someone else.

Active Listening. This involves genuinely listening to and understanding another's viewpoint without interrupting or making assumptions. You can seek clarification by asking, "Am I correct in understanding that you're concerned about...?"

Verbal and Non-Verbal Congruence. Your words, tone, and facial expressions should be in harmony. When talking about your disappointment, use a sad expression rather than an angry one.

Questioning. This helps clarify the other party's stance and demonstrates your interest. For instance: "What exactly did you mean when you said...?"

Ability to Say "No". Confidence in setting boundaries. "I understand where you're coming from, but I can't do that." This showcases respect for yourself and your limits.

Seeking Compromise, if Possible. Aim for a solution that is agreeable to both parties. "Let's try to find a solution that works for both of us."

Being Direct. Openly and honestly expressing feelings and needs. "I would have appreciated it if you had informed me earlier," especially when someone alters agreed-upon terms midway.

Stay Calm. The capability to manage your emotions, even under pressure. Speak in a confident yet calm tone, even if the person you're conversing with becomes aggressive.

When employing assertive skills in conflict situations, it's vital to remember that the goal isn't to "win" the argument but to convey your position while respecting the other's viewpoint. In any case, be conscious of your personal boundaries, wishes, and interests. Don't let bullies provoke you. Resort to aggression or flight only if your life is in immediate danger. Most conflicts are trivial and are meant merely to provoke.

CHAPTER NINE

Artificial Surplus.

Artificial social scarcity is a phenomenon where society or a particular group creates the notion of a shortage of something they believe is essential to meet societal standards or ideals. Interestingly, this perceived scarcity might not exist in reality or might not be as critical as portrayed.

Examples of artificially induced societal scarcities include:

1. Fashion Trends. Clothing and accessory brands often induce an artificial scarcity by releasing "limited editions." This gives an illusion of rarity and exclusivity, urging people to purchase at higher prices and within a shorter span.

2. Beauty Standards. Media and advertising are known to set artificial beauty standards. This can lead to a sense of deficiency among those who don't match up, fueling the popularity of cosmetic surgeries, diets, and other enhancements.

3. Status Symbols. Makers of luxury goods like cars or watches frequently generate artificial scarcity by launching "limited series," adding a premium price and status to these items.

4. Education. In some countries, there's a contrived shortage of seats in prestigious institutions, leading to competition, added tests, and costly preparation.

5. Housing. Big cities can witness an artificial housing shortage, leading to escalating rent and property purchase prices.

The concept of artificial scarcity is deeply rooted in human psychology. The mere feeling of scarcity can trigger a desire to secure a rare resource, even if it's not vital.

This is often linked to societal pressures and the urge to conform to societal norms or to stand out among peers.

Look for Places Where You're in High Demand. Every skill consists of a series of actions. Similarly, the art of achieving success and happiness is based on certain behavioral traits. Being in the right place at the right time is one of the key ones.

This principle is built upon the idea of seeking out situations where your skills, experience, or mere presence is valued more than usual. By finding such "hotspots" or areas with a high demand for you, you can boost your self-confidence, social standing, and even career prospects.

Take the example of a guy in a dance class—it's a classic case. In most dance classes, there are usually more women than men, making men much sought after. This might provide the man with more opportunities to practice, choose a dance partner, and potentially elevate his social standing within the group. Here are some other examples:

1. Specialist in a niche area. If you're an expert in a rare or specialized field, your expertise might be in high demand in certain companies or industries.

2. A foreigner proficient in their native language. Living abroad and speaking your native tongue? You might find yourself in demand in schools, universities, or companies looking for translators or teachers.

3. A rare skill in your community. Let's say you can repair specific types of machinery or devices, and there aren't many specialists in your town. You'll likely be in high demand.

4. An athlete in a school team. If you possess unique sports skills and you move to a school that's lacking such talent, you might be welcomed with open arms.

5. A musician in a small town. If you play an instrument well and move to a small town lacking many musicians, you'll quickly become popular and sought-after.

6. Volunteer with a medical background. If you're volunteering in a region where there's a shortage of medical practitioners, your skills will be worth their weight in gold.

7. Educator in a children's camp. If you have experience working with children and the camp lacks adults who can conduct intriguing workshops or entertainments, you'll become a "star" amongst both the organizers and the children.

8. Handcraft artisan. In the digital age, the ability to create with one's hands is becoming increasingly rare. If you're skilled in crafts like knitting, sewing, or pottery, you could be a sensation in certain communities.

9. Digital tech-savvy senior. Many older individuals feel lost in today's tech-driven world. If you're of that age but understand computers, smartphones, and the internet, your knowledge will be in demand amongst your peers.

In every place and every situation, there's something unique you can offer, whether it's your experience, skill, or mere presence. Find your "hotspot" and leverage it to your advantage.

This skill also extends to everyday domestic situations, which form a large part of our lives. Being in the right place at the right time is not just about luck or fate but also the result of skill in evaluating the environment and managing time efficiently.

Evaluate your surroundings. Regularly analyzing both your professional and personal environments allows you to anticipate events and stay a step ahead. For instance, if you're aware that your city hosts cultural events on every last Friday of the month, by keeping an eye on event listings, you'll not only attend something you enjoy but might also bump into an old friend attending the same.

Flexibility and adaptability. Being ready for change and responding to it quickly is vital for positioning yourself advantageously.

Listen to your intuition. Sometimes, your inner self might have cues on where to go or what to do. Like, on a whim, you might decide to visit a bookstore instead of heading straight home and discover a book you've been longing to read, now on sale.

Networking. The broader your social network, the more opportunities you have to be in the right place at the right time. Your friends might inform you about a surprise gig of your favorite band in a local bar. With that knowledge, you get to be there and enjoy the performance.

Planning and Forecasting. The better you plan your day or week, the higher the chance you'll be in the right place when it counts. Knowing that shells often appear on your favorite beach after the rain, you might decide to head there and find a rare specimen for your collection. All it takes is a quick check of the weather forecast and setting aside time for the trip.

Being in the right place at the right time is a mix of intuition, planning, social connections, and adaptability. It's essential to combine these elements to carve out fortunate moments for oneself. Even in mundane situations, this skill can make life more fulfilling and harmonious.

Many successful individuals who have reached great heights in their careers or life in general had the knack for being in the right place at the right time. But it's crucial to recognize that often behind such "luck" is a lot of hard work, analysis, and planning. Here are some notable personalities as examples:

1. Bill Gates. As a youngster, Gates got access to a computer at his school and spent a considerable amount of time learning programming. When IBM was looking for a company to develop an OS for their first PC, Gates and Microsoft were poised

to provide a solution, which ultimately led to the creation of MS-DOS and subsequently Windows.

2. Steve Jobs. While attending a calligraphy class at Reed College, Jobs was introduced to the principles of typography. This experience later influenced the design of Apple computers, setting them apart visually.

3. Oprah Winfrey. After years in radio and television, Oprah became the host of a morning talk show in Chicago. Her unique approach to interviews and her empathetic nature made her rapidly popular, leading to her very own talk show.

4. Walt Disney. Walt visited an exhibition where he saw miniature mechanical figures, inspiring the idea for Disneyland. He located the right piece of land and subsequently built his first theme park.

5. J.K. Rowling. Despite numerous personal challenges, Rowling never gave up on her dream of becoming an author. When she wrote the first Harry Potter book, she was in the right place at the right time, as the world was looking for a unique children's book that would appeal to adults too.

These examples underline that being at the right place at the right time often goes hand in hand with a readiness to take risks, self-belief, and persistence.

CHAPTER TEN

The Power of Unity.

Jim's work on the mural was complete, and tomorrow the jury would evaluate the creations of the participants and decide on the winner. Throughout the two weeks he worked on the mural, Jim and Rachel would often stroll past that wall to take a look. And so it was on this evening.

"You did it, Jim," she whispered, leaning into his shoulder. "It's truly amazing."

Jim smiled, feeling his cheeks flush with pride. "Thank you, Rach. But without your support, it would've been much harder."

"Nervous about the jury's decision tomorrow?" Rachel asked.

"It doesn't seem like it," he said after a brief pause. At that moment, the decision was inconsequential for Jim. What mattered most was the realization that he'd seen his work through, overcoming every challenge.

"Do you remember how I doubted myself at the beginning?" he asked, looking deep into Rachel's eyes.

She nodded. "Yes, and I'm proud of how you dealt with it. Not only did you create a remarkable mural, but you also showed me that bravery and persistence can overcome any obstacle."

Jim chuckled, "I think it was the same persistence that helped me deal with Larry at the hardware store."

Rachel laughed too. "Perhaps. But I'm glad you resisted the urge to get into a fight. This mural is far more important."

The Secrets of Living

Walking hand in hand, Jim and Rachel passed by stores, cafes, and parks, heading towards the wall featuring the mural. The streets were bathed in a warm evening glow, and the hum of city life echoed around them.

"You know, Jim," Rachel began, "when I think about all the effort you poured into this mural, I feel such immense pride for you."

Jim smiled, glancing at her. "Thanks, Rach. But you know, it wasn't just my achievement. This project allowed me to express myself, yes, but it also showed how significant people like you are to me."

Rachel blushed. "I'm curious about what additions you made to the mural since I last saw it."

"Oh, I made a few enhancements," Jim smirked. "You'll know when you see it."

Rachel winked at him. "I've always loved surprises."

They continued their walk, basking in each other's company.

"Who do you think will win the contest?" Rachel asked, looking ahead thoughtfully.

"I don't know," replied Jim, "Many of the participants are talented. But for me, winning isn't the primary goal in this project; it's the journey. You were right when you said that I needed to at least try and gain experience. I feel like I've grown and evolved while creating this mural. But I'm also very pleased with the outcome."

Rachel nodded, "I get you. Sometimes the journey is more significant than the end result."

As they neared the mural, they noticed flashing red and blue lights from police cars in the distance. With each step, the flashing became more pronounced. The atmosphere grew tense.

Jim and Rachel slowed down as they realized that their meticulously crafted mural had been defaced. Large streaks of red paint marred the image, blurring and distorting the carefully crafted details. It looked like bloody tears that were washing away Jim's creation.

Feeling Jim's legs falter from shock, Rachel tightly gripped his hand. "Jim... this is horrific," she whispered.

Jim, unable to muster any words, just nodded. His face was pale, and his eyes were filled with pain.

Several police officers stood by the mural, discussing the incident. One of them approached the couple. "Do you know anything about this?"

Gathering his composure, Jim replied, "Yes, it's my work. I spent weeks on it."

The officer nodded. "We're truly sorry. We were patrolling the area and spotted suspicious-looking guy in some sort of robe; he had a large utility bag with him. The officer pointed to the bag on the ground. "He was already here when we pulled up and asked him what he was doing. Before we could even step out of the car, he quickly pulled out a paint can and splashed the mural. We detained him immediately. It's fortunate we were passing by because, judging by the number of paint cans, he planned to douse the entire mural. Only a small portion, mainly on the side, was affected."

Jim was speechless, and the officer looked at him sympathetically, "We're really sorry, sir."

"But who did this, and why?" Jim's voice quivered, closer to a whimper than question.

"The suspect is in the back seat of our car." The officer walked beside Jim, ready to restrain him should his grief turn aggressive.

The Secrets of Living

Approaching the police car, Jim caught sight of a young man, about twenty years old. He had a distant look in his eyes, and a smirk played on his lips. There was no doubt he relished in his act of destruction.

"Do you know him?" inquired the officer.

Rachel, taking a closer look, shuddered. "That's Larry, Jim's classmate. He was always mean and envious."

Larry's smirk remained. As Jim stared at him, disbelief etched into every feature, words failed him entirely. Then Larry's voice brought him crashing back to reality: "We meet again, Jimmy."

They moved slightly away from the police car, and Rachel wrapped her arms around Jim's shoulders, sensing the tremor that ran through his body from the shock.

"I spent so much time on that piece," Jim began, desperation evident in his voice. "Now it's all ruined. I can't compete in the contest anymore."

"Jim, I get how hard this is," Rachel said, her gaze locked onto his. "But we can still make something out of this. You're a talented artist, and I believe you can rebuild your work."

"It's beyond repair, Rachel," Jim replied, the desolation heavy in his tone. "Even if I had the time, it'll never be the same. I put a part of myself into it, and now it's all torn apart."

"Listen to me," Rachel said confidently. "We can always find a way out. Perhaps this is a chance for you to see your creation in a new light and create something even more extraordinary."

Jim stared at her, as if trying to grasp her meaning. "What are you suggesting?"

"We can use what happened as a part of the art," Rachel explained. "What Larry did can symbolize how life can hit us unexpectedly, but it doesn't mean we can't rise up and create something anew."

Jim looked thoughtful, staring at his ruined work. "You think that could actually work?"

Rachel smiled, "You have every chance to make it work. You're an incredible artist, and I believe you'll find a way to turn this incident into something special."

Jim took a deep breath, "Thanks, Rachel. I'll try. But first, I need some time to process all of this."

Rachel hugged him. "You don't have the luxury of time right now. The judges will be here by noon tomorrow. Let's think about what we can fix, what adjustments are needed."

"I have an idea," Jim replied. "The main spilled section, I can stylize it to look like an old brick wall. That shouldn't take too long. The other splatters can be painted over with the original colors."

"That's a great idea!" Rachel exclaimed with joy.

Jim lowered his head, "The idea might be great, but there's not enough time until tomorrow, and the lighting is poor."

"There might not be enough time for you and me, but you have friends from art courses and the painter's crew. They can help, and I bet your crew has powerful lighting for painting jobs, to spot wall imperfections and such."

Jim looked at her in surprise. "You really think they'd come to help at this late hour?"

Laughing, Rachel replied, "Of course! You have no idea how inspiring you are to many of them. Not to mention they all owe you one – you've helped them out in various situations. It's worth a shot."

"Alright," said Jim, beginning to sound more spirited, "let's try to assemble a team. I need to start making calls."

Rachel nodded. "Meanwhile, I'll fetch the remaining paints from my studio. Plus, I have contacts with the contest organizers; perhaps they can provide additional lighting."

With that, they both set to their tasks.

A few hours later, around Jim's damaged work, a whole team had gathered. Young individuals, brushes and paints in hand, ready to work, stood before the marred piece.

"Now that's what I call a team!" Jim said, looking at all his friends who'd come to help. "I didn't expect all of you to show up."

"C'mon, Jim!" one of the friends countered. "You've helped us out countless times. It's our turn to return the favor!"

Rachel approached Jim with a basket full of paints and handed him a brush. "Shall we begin?"

Jim nodded and flicked the switch. Powerful spotlights, set up near the wall, illuminated every nook and cranny. Soon, the air was filled with the sounds of brushes and aerosol sprays. Everyone worked in harmony, complementing one another as if they were one entity. Thanks to their collective effort, the restoration process was much swifter than Jim could have ever imagined.

As dawn approached, a nearly completed masterpiece stood before them. It had been given a new lease of life, all thanks to the efforts of those present. Now, it looked even more vibrant and expressive than before.

"Thank you all," Jim voiced, addressing everyone. "I could never have done this on my own. You truly are the best friends anyone could ask for."

Everyone, though exhausted, responded with smiles. Rachel approached Jim and embraced him. "See, I told you we could do it."

Jim grinned back, "Yes, thanks to you and all our friends. Together, we can achieve the impossible."

Human as a Social Animal.

The great philosopher Aristotle once remarked, "Human is by nature a social animal." Centuries have passed since then, but these words remain as relevant as ever. Human nature inherently involves living in communities and interacting with others. Such interaction is not merely desirable but absolutely essential.

Without social interaction, we wither. This isn't mere metaphor, it's a reality. A lack of social connections can lead to stress, depression, and even physical ailments. Loneliness isn't just a feeling of emptiness; it poses a genuine threat to our health. Clinical studies have shown that prolonged isolation can reduce life expectancy as much as smoking or obesity does.

But communication is about more than avoiding solitude. It's also about mutual assistance. In ancient times, humans grouped into tribes to survive, hunt, and defend against predators. Today, despite technological advancements, we still rely on each other. Each one of us seeks support—sometimes physical, but often emotional.

Conversely, humans have a need to assist others. This isn't just an act of altruism; it's also a way to affirm one's value to the community. Helping another brings satisfaction, a sense of purpose, and a feeling of life's worth.

Ultimately, every individual craves recognition. We yearn for our contributions to be valued, our achievements acknowledged. Such recognition reassures us that our efforts, sacrifices, and virtues matter to others. It bolsters our self-confidence and drives us forward. Our quest for communication, mutual assistance, and acknowledgment forms the bedrock of our humanity. It's what defines us. It's what makes our world so special and unique.

For ages, people from every corner of the earth have aided one another, deeply embedding this practice into our cultural and moral values. Assisting others isn't just an act—it's a reflection of our inner selves, our stance towards society, and our relationship with our own persona.

Primarily, when we help others, we broaden our horizons. This allows us to see the world through another person's eyes, understanding their needs and feelings. Offering aid unveils a world potentially much broader and diverse than our personal experiences.

Furthermore, assisting others strengthens our sense of solidarity. It reminds us that, regardless of our individual differences, we are all interdependent. During trying times, this is particularly vital, as solidarity fosters the creation of robust, resilient communities capable of confronting any adversity.

Helping also serves as a catalyst for personal growth. By addressing others' issues, we cultivate compassion, tolerance, and gratitude. These attributes render us more whole, more aware, and more attuned to the needs of those around us.

Helping isn't merely a donation of resources or time. It represents the pinnacle of human activity, enhancing our interconnections and rendering our world richer and more harmonious. It signifies a conscious choice to be an active participant in societal life, opting to be a beacon of goodness in a world that sorely requires it.

If we inherently crave social interactions, let's make them as beneficial as possible. Which friends and acquaintances could be valuable?

Human relationships play a pivotal role in our lives. They enrich our experience and catalyze our growth and development. However, if we aim to make our social interactions as fruitful and productive as possible, it's crucial to surround ourselves with a diverse set of friends and acquaintances. Here are several categories of people that could prove invaluable:

1. Mentors and guides. Individuals who can offer sage advice, teach you new skills, or share their experiences. They will help you envision possibilities and understand pathways to achieve your aspirations.

2. Professional friends. Having friends specialized in various fields (like a lawyer, doctor, artisan, IT specialist, etc.) can prove beneficial in everyday life.

3. Creative minds. Those constantly seeking fresh ideas and solutions can inspire you towards new ventures and projects.

4. Critics. As long as their feedback is constructive, such individuals will help you recognize the weak spots in your approaches or ideas and suggest avenues for enhancement.

5. Positive and Optimistic Individuals. Their upbeat attitude can be infectious, especially during challenging times.

6. Networkers. Those who have a broad range of acquaintances across different areas can help you expand your social circle or locate necessary resources.

7. Listener Friends. Sometimes you just need to vent, and these friends are always ready to listen.

8. People with Alternative Viewpoints. They can provide a different perspective or make you think about matters you haven't previously considered.

Ideally, your social circle should represent a mix of all these types of people. Such diversity enriches your life, offers new opportunities, and renders your social interactions most beneficial.

To be of value to others and, in turn, count on their assistance, several key principles should be considered:

1. Be Genuine. Nothing is valued more than sincerity. Help others without immediately expecting a favor in return. Such acts earn respect and elicit a desire to reciprocate.

2. Hone Your Skills. The more you know and can do, the more opportunities you have to assist others. Continuous learning and development make you a valued asset in your field.

3. Listen and Understand. At times, the best way to help is simply to listen. Understand what a person specifically requires, and extend your aid accordingly.

4. Be Reliable. If you've committed to assisting, fulfill your promise. Reliability establishes a reputation as someone trustworthy.

5. Cultivate and Maintain a Network. Engaging with various individuals augments your resource pool. In the future, you might bridge connections, aiding them in problem-solving.

6. Don't Hesitate to Ask for Help. When facing difficulties, don't be shy about reaching out. This demonstrates that you value others' expertise and skills.

7. Treat People with Respect. Always honor the time, opinions, and resources of others. Showcase that you appreciate their contributions.

8. Maintain the Connection. Even a simple "thank you" or a brief message can sustain a relationship. At times, small gestures hold significant importance.

9. Share Your Resources. If you possess something that might benefit another person (information, contacts, skills), don't hesitate to share.

10. Offer Assistance. Some people might be too shy to ask, but if you extend your help, it could be precisely what they need.

A continuous desire to be useful and readiness to offer support fosters an atmosphere of mutual assistance. When you perform acts of kindness without expecting a reward, people sense it and typically aspire to reciprocate.

Profound, genuine relationships and friendships cannot be solely measured by practical utility or possession of certain skills. Often, the most precious moments in life are the simple knowledge that there's someone ready to stand by you during tough times, offering support in words or deeds.

Friends who are willing to lend a hand not for some benefits but because they truly value you are a real treasure. Such relationships demand time, attention, and effort to maintain, but they're worth it. Mutual respect, trust, and genuine care fortify the bonds, making them resilient to life's storms.

Hence, it's essential to dedicate time to your friends, show interest in their lives, celebrate their achievements, and support them during challenging periods. It's such bonds that will bring you the most joy and satisfaction in life.

Always remember, having friends, even if their skills and knowledge might not seem directly essential to you, but who genuinely stand ready to help at any given moment, is an invaluable asset. Cherish such relationships.

Let's Summarize

Dear readers, this book was crafted with the hope of inspiring you on a journey to become the best version of yourself. Life often presents us with challenges, doubts, and uncertainties, but as you've discovered, each of us possesses inexhaustible potential for growth and development.

The art of achieving success and happiness can be roughly divided into a series of key actions or habits:

1. Goal Setting: Defining and understanding what you want to achieve in life, then creating a specific plan to reach it.

2. Lifelong Learning: Recognizing that the world is constantly changing and having the desire to learn and grow with it.

3. Hard Work: Mastering any skill by repeating it until it becomes second nature, making it an integral part of you.

4. Reflection: Regularly assessing your actions and results to understand what can be improved.

5. Time Management: Efficiently allocating your time to tasks that bring you closer to your goals.

6. Positive Thinking: Focusing on the positive aspects of life and using them as a source of motivation.

7. Setting Boundaries: Understanding your personal limits and the ability to say "no" to distractions from your goals.

8. Overcoming Failure: Recognizing that failures are temporary and provide an opportunity for learning.

9. Self-Discipline: The ability to motivate yourself to complete necessary tasks, even if they don't bring immediate joy.

10. Building Social Connections: Establishing and maintaining relationships with people who support your goals and values.

11. The Ability to Be in the Right Place at the Right Time.

These habits and actions can help create a foundation for a successful and happy life. Of course, every person is unique, and what works for one may not suit another. The key is to adapt and apply these principles in a way that resonates with your individual journey.

Remember, personal growth is not a destination but a continuous journey. Embrace each step, cherish the progress, and never stop seeking the best version of yourself. You have the potential to achieve greatness, and this book is your guide on that remarkable journey.

The importance of self-esteem and the factors upon which it is built and sustained cannot be precisely measured. We cannot definitively say how much it affects your happiness and success. However, when you are in a bad mood, the likelihood of engaging with someone in a good mood decreases. You may possess the necessary skills, but with low self-esteem, you won't be able to effectively utilize them. It is also true that without a specific skill but with high self-esteem and self-confidence, you are more likely to dare to acquire that skill when needed. The probability of making friends, seeking a good job, engaging in creative experiments, traveling, creatively reevaluating everyday things and problem-solving, exercising the right to refuse, and critically perceiving information while safeguarding your personal boundaries - all of these events are more likely to happen with self-assurance.

As soon as you start trying to do things and take actions that you may have previously avoided for various reasons, your self-belief will also begin to grow. Initially, by making conscious efforts, if required, you initiate a process of change that can no longer be stopped.

I want to express my gratitude to my parents who laid the foundation and nurtured my skills; to my teachers, no matter how challenging their job, they did it professionally and passionately; to my colleagues, always ready to offer advice in difficult situations; to clients who trusted me and allowed me to help; to my beloved friends, you are always there, filling my life with happiness; dear reader, thank you for choosing this book, I hope our time together was beneficial for you, and I hope our friendship lasts for many years, I am grateful to you because it was you who motivated me to write this book; to my Significant Other, first and foremost, I am grateful to fate for bringing us together, you are always there, helping me, being with you is the best gift for me.

Printed in Great Britain
by Amazon